THE RIVER LINE

"THE RIVER LINE"
A PLAY

by

CHARLES MORGAN

'We must act like men who have the enemy
at their gates, and at the same time like men
who are working for eternity.'
MAZZINI, *during the Defence of Rome, 1849*

LONDON
MACMILLAN & CO. LTD
1952

TO THE MEMORY OF

HILARY ST. GEORGE SAUNDERS

for the pleasure of recalling that our
friendship of more than thirty years
began, when we were undergraduate
actors, on the field of Corunna and
in the Forest of Arden.

> *Sir, fare you well;*
> *Hereafter, in a better world than this,*
> *I shall desire more love and knowledge of you.*

HIS EXIT LINES AS LE BEAU

If I but had the eyes and ears
To read within what now appears,
Then should I see in every face
An innocent, interior grace,
And, as the clouds of thought unfurled,
Be native of the golden world.

For not by thought shall I acquire
Re-entrance to my heart's desire,
Nor as a ticket-tourist come
Out of exile to my own home.

All things that are of Earth or Hell
We gain or lose and buy or sell,
But Heaven's deep-enclosed delight
Is an hereditary right
Which this man's lust nor that man's hate
Nor my cold sin can alienate,
But lives my own, when all else dies,
Within my blood, within my eyes :
So true it is that my dis-Grace
Is absence from my Native Place.

INTRODUCTION

ON TRANSCENDING THE AGE OF VIOLENCE

THE origin, or what Henry James would have called 'the germ', of *The River Line* is clear in my recollection: it was the phrase *un faux Anglais*, a sham Englishman, which I first heard spoken in Paris, within a few weeks of the Liberation, in the context of the Resistance Movement.

While Europe lay under the German yoke, there had sprung up certain organizations of valiant men and women, Belgian and French, which enabled Americans and English, who had escaped from German prisons or been shot down from the air over occupied territory, to make their way home. These organizations, or 'lines', had something in common with the coaching system of our ancestors. A little group of allied fugitives would be passed on from post to post, through Belgium, through France, into Spain, and each post was someone's home, where, at the utmost peril of its inhabitants, these human 'parcels' were hidden until they could be moved forward.

How cruel the danger was to the French and Belgian guardians of our men, we English and Americans do not easily understand, for, though we have suffered other things, we have not had the enemy sitting in our chairs and swarming in our streets. Nor have our countries been submitted to those conditions which breed collaborators and set friend against friend. The guardians in these escape-lines had everything to fear, week after week, month after month. They had not even the refuge of the *maquis*. They had all to perform the normal duties of their domestic and professional lives and, at the same time, to accept the steely discipline of a secret agent. It is one thing to leave civilian life, to put on uniform, and to go into battle openly in the companionship of friends ; it is altogether another to admit the abominations of violence and clandestinity into your own home, to lie down with them each night and awake to them each morning, and, in the isolation that security imposes, to trust no one, to guard perpetually each impulse of eye or tongue.

So these men and women lived and worked. I will not say that their courage was greater than the courage of soldiers in the field, only that it was different and fills me with a special awe. It was unfortified by the discipline of ship or regiment. These hermits of the Resistance could not live, as members of an enclosed religious order live, in a community of their devotion, and were at the same time without even such freedom of movement as may be the salvation of a secret agent, who, when one place becomes too hot for him, may at least seek another. They were rooted in their own place, bound to preserve before their neighbours the appearances of normal life, while their homes, and their minds inevitably, were invaded by the extreme abnormality, the vicious and absurd and irrational melodrama, of our age of violence. Their suffering must have been more than bodily fear of discovery and its consequences. It must have seemed to many of them, in the dark night of this experience, that they and the fugitives they succoured and the Germans themselves were but dust in a God-abandoned world. Often they must have felt, in the proportion of the war, that their task did not make sense and that their courage was running to waste. Nevertheless they endured through the years; and I acknowledge that their devoted and solitary duty has for me an aspect of saintliness which none of us, who were trained in the regular Services, would claim for his own.

2

The existence of these secret escape-lines was, of course, well known to us long before the Liberation. From time to time a post would be mopped up and its guardian vanish, but another post would replace it. The line was diverted, not destroyed, and the flow of escape continued.

Often I would wonder which of my French friends were engaged in this service. In thinking of them, I had always supposed that, as guardians of a post, their danger would spring from two sources only: from the Germans and from collaborators, both external to their own homes. It did not occur to me that they had anything to fear from the officers and men who passed through their hands. Were not these fugitives American or British? Was not their interest identical with that of their French guardians? What was to be feared from them? And yet I was to learn that fear of betrayal from within was the fear that overrode all others in the escape-lines. The name of this fear was '*un faux Anglais*'.

This was taught me in Paris on an August day of 1944. The enemy had but recently been driven out, and Paris was happy as I have never known a city be happy before or since, not with wild rejoicing but with profound and passionate relief. I was, I believe, the only civilian and unofficial Englishman to have reached France so early, and the French, expecting nothing but soldiers and more soldiers, looked at an English writer in plain clothes as though he were a visitor from another world.

Memory of those re-encounters will never fade while I live : how eyes widened and held their gaze like the eyes of children ; how hand clung to hand, feeling with incredulous avidity the living flesh and bones ; how even the sun, and wine in the glass, were as wine and sun had never been before. There was the shiver of renaissance in the air. Little more than two months later, when I came to Paris again for the reopening of the Comédie-Française, the sense of relief remained, but the French were already settling down to the business of existence. They had resumed their eternal task of analysis and self-criticism ; they were correcting and re-correcting the prose of life ; the freshness, the lyricism of the early days was gone.

How wonderful it had been then to ask after an old friend and to receive, not the common answer : 'He is well', but the August answer : 'He is alive '! I for my friends, my friends for me, were all in that hour young again and newly risen from the grave. There before our eyes was Paris, a French Paris, and there, as astonishing evidence of how Germans hope to conciliate those whom they mean to destroy, was L'Aiglon beside his father in the Invalides; it was pleasant to watch a Frenchman smile at that. . . . And there were the river and the Ile St.-Louis and the rue Bonaparte and the rue de Seine and the little house at Vanves, and no Germans. The river flowed down to Mantes, to La Roche Guyon, to Vernon, to Rouen, to the sea, and there were ruins, but no Germans. The air was sweet with their absence. It was French air. One might talk above a whisper with one's friends.

3

One of these, whom even now I will not name lest another time come, taught me much of the escape-lines.

'What we had most to fear,' he said, 'was *un faux Anglais*.'

I mistranslated: 'A false Englishman?'

'No,' he replied with a swift glance, 'a sham one.'

The Germans, he explained, had known that his escape-line existed, but not how it worked. Each post in the line was, as much as possible, localized. He himself had known little outside his own area; there was not much that even under torture he could have given away, and this had been true, except in rare instances, of those who had been captured. Even when a leader with wider knowledge had been taken, the enemy had not guessed her importance; they had been content to flog and imprison as a matter of routine, and had missed their opportunity for what my friend called 'a refined interrogation'.

Taught at last by disappointment that to pluck out a link here and there did not enable them to destroy the chain, the Germans had adopted (or so it was believed) a more elaborate plan. They would, if they could, introduce into the escape-line an agent of theirs specially qualified and trained to pose as an escaping Englishman. Together with his genuine companions, he would be passed on from post to post, carefully observing each. Once beyond the Pyrenees, he would vanish and report back to his headquarters. The whole escape-line would be swept up in concerted raids.

For this reason, every escaper passing through their homes was suspect to the French — the more so because, when he was genuine, he might often be without secure evidence of identity, and because evidence, if the Germans used material drawn from their prison-camps or from the dead, could be accurately counterfeited.

As my friend told me this, I understood how reasonable and pervasive had been the French dread of *un faux Anglais*. At first, I remember, I saw the possible story from the point of view of a German agent thus introduced into an escape-line. His family would be English on his mother's side, he would have received an English education and have spent a great part of his life among us ; he would have to be one of those exceedingly rare foreigners whose conversation is not only fluent, correct, and without accent, but has the slackness, the slur, the clipping or the drawing-out of syllables which make it indistinguishable from the conversation of Englishmen themselves. Even with this flawless ease of language to give him cover, a sham Englishman, living at close quarters with genuine Englishmen in granaries and box-rooms, would be in unceasing danger. He could not, in the nature of the case, have lived in England recently; there would be gaps in whatever personal or regimental background he had chosen to assume; and as he came to know and like his companions, and to be known and liked by them, the risk of his giving himself away by the use of a wrong name or by failure to grasp a fragment of new military slang, would increase. It was true that discovery would mean for him death only, and not torture, as it might for the French. Even so, his solitude would be greater than theirs and the skill required of him more complex. He, too, would be a dedicated man, and I began imaginatively to enter into him, to see with his eyes, to think with his brain, to touch with his fingers, and to remember, with his memory, passages of his childhood in the light of which the service that now compelled him was an aberration — the same aberration, at once hideous and heroic, as that of his French guardians and his English companions; the aberration, like a nightmare, that may exact from any one of us in the age of violence a self-immolation magnificent in itself, and yet irrational and perverse. Only a fool without knowledge of the absolutism of service would speak of a spy as 'cowardly', and yet the performance of his duty rests upon the winning and the betrayal of trust; it is a perversion of life's good; and I had assumed, in thinking of my German, that he would be aware of this as Narwitz in *The Fountain* would have been aware. Suddenly I doubted it. Narwitz had belonged to the old Germany; he had read Turgenev with love; he had had a gentle power to make those distinctions of taste and conscience which totalitarianism excludes; and I remembered that it was Bernstorff, icily contemptuous of the Nazis for this very reason, who, at Aix, had been pleased and surprised that a young Englishman had written a just portrait of a Prussian aristocrat. A Nazi agent in 1943 was likely to be an altogether different animal, with a mob-mind beyond the range of my sympathy, and I recoiled from the thought of his being the protagonist of my drama.

For what had appeared in the half-light where stories wait to be born was a play, not a novel. In that sense, the present play is far from being an adaptation or dramatization of my novel of the same name. Rather was the novel, in effect, a study for the play, written because for a time the structure of the play eluded me.

The scene, as I first saw it, was to be the Chassaignes' granary throughout, and the pivot of the action fear of *un faux Anglais*. But an obstacle at once appeared. I did not see how to communicate this fear in the theatre without making the Nazi, if not the protagonist, at least a principal character, of my tale, and I knew in my heart that, however much I might admire his courage, however stringently I might in my intellect accept his dedication as being for him valid, I was yet not in charity with him as a writer must be in charity even with his enemy characters, if he is — I will not say if he is to give life to them, but if he is to accept life from them. Knowing that my heart was hardened against my Nazi agent, not because he was German but because I could not imaginatively penetrate as I ought the mask and mechanism of a totalitarian mind, I knew that I must not write of him. Hardness of heart is a sterilizing sin in literature as in life. It is a will to excommunicate, and none of us, in his capacity of human being and least of all in his capacity of dramatist, has the power or the right to excommunicate. Shakespeare did not excommunicate Shylock or Iago ; he entered into them, suffered with them ; they are therefore men, not monsters ; and it is remarkable that to the extent that Shakespeare did from time to time harden his heart against Iago, to that same extent is Iago from time to time unacceptably monstrous.

It was, therefore, plain that, though I had written of Narwitz, who also was a German and an enemy, I was not able, I was not yet fit, to write of my Nazi agent because I could not see his innocence through his guilt. And for a long time it seemed impossible to write my play without him. On what other figure than his could the fear of *un faux Anglais* be projected ?

4

Two things then happened. First, the figure of Heron emerged, not only as a substitute for the Nazi agent and one who, from the point of view of a story-teller, was usefully double-edged, but as a character to whom I was naturally drawn by his vigour in action and his quietness in thought. I liked him because he was not restive in this angry world and yet was not a crank.

Next, and as a consequence, the play deepened. I saw that the fear of *un faux Anglais* was only the occasion of its action and not its theme. Its theme, to be considered in the light of each of its characters, all converging upon Heron and reflected back by him, was the predicament of us all who, being men and women of peaceful mind nurtured in a rule of law derived from ancient Rome and tempered by Christian emphasis upon *each* man's inalienable worth and responsibility as the child of God, find ourselves in a world where great hordes have rejected, or have never learned, the traditions of Rome and of Christ, of Athens and of the Renaissance, and are determined to wipe away even the memory of them from the earth. Where, in these circumstances, does our responsibility lie? Would not the great doctrine of non-resistance have presented new aspects to Tolstoy himself if he had been living now? Are we not bound to resist? If so, with what weapons and in what spirit? And if, using against the hordes their own weapons of clandestinity and violence, we kill unknowingly, as Philip and Marie and Julian did, the thing we love, how shall we be absolved? So I began to see the violent action in the Chassaignes' granary, and its consequences in the lives of those who took part in it, as action and consequence that at least asked certain questions which, though the questions themselves are as old as conscience, have to be re-stated in the contemporary mind.

Here another obstacle arose to my treating the subject in a play. I had become concerned not only with the action in the French granary but with its consequences at long-term, not only with 1943 but with 1947; and I could not see how to interlace the two periods, the cause and the consequence, without writing a play of the episodic kind to which the conditions of our theatre are unfriendly. Except in the great leisure and looseness of the Elizabethan stage, one cannot divide and subdivide a dramatic structure without permitting illusion to drain away through the cracks ; and I could hit upon no device that would keep the scene-shifters at bay and allow me my retrospect. The freer convention of a novel seemed inevitable, but I accepted it with a hankering after my lost play. Years were to pass before I heard Philip Sturgess begin to tell the story of his French adventure as he left an English garden at the end of Act I, and saw how the truth and its consequences might pour in upon him in Act III, leaving the River Line episode in a firm bracket, to be what it had always been — the narrative's core.

These are technical matters of greater interest, perhaps, to a writer than to a spectator of plays, and I will say no more of them than that they confirmed my long-held belief that when, in planning a tale or living a life, one encounters a locked door, it is as well not at once to force the lock but to turn aside from it, to do something else, to go to sleep perhaps, and to wait ; for in the end, if we do not rattle and bang, doors often open themselves that have anything for us on the other side. And if there is nothing on their other side that we are capable of receiving naturally and tranquilly, it is as well that they should remain shut. A great part of the world's energy has been spent in breaking into prison. In the end, all violence proves itself to have been unintelligent.

In the end . . . But meanwhile how shall we live in an age of violence ? With infinite subtlety, the question presents itself in a different aspect to each of us — to Julian, for whom it is, in a measure, simplified by the overriding tradition of his naval service, and who has been, in equal measure, hardened by his over-simplification; to Marie Chassaigne, for whom, as a woman essentially ordered and rational, it is a question of how to preserve the natural reason of her French inheritance — its repugnance to hysterical extremes, to the fantastic and the obsessed — and yet, at the same time, to fight with clandestine weapons, the only weapons available to her, the disease of sadistic sentimentality which, in the form of Nazi invasion, afflicts her country; to young Frewer, who is bewildered and finds in Heron's acceptances a focus for his mind's eye ; and to Philip Sturgess, an American, kind, sensitive, and no shirker of his part in the human tragedy, who yet, because he is of the New World and has been bred in its hopes of perfectibility, is inclined at first to regard the violence that torments the Old as an unreal devil which the educative and electoral processes might comfortably exorcize. The climate of his thought when he is plunged into the age of violence is different from ours, for he has indeed been plunged into it from the outside, whereas it has grown up around us like a miasma, it is a poison in the air we breathe arising from a corruption of the idea of democracy. The strength of Philip Sturgess is that, when the facts are known to him, he adjusts his ideas to them. He accepts personal responsibility for what he has done, though he did it under a misapprehension; he has none of the facility for collective self-excuse and self-forgiveness and self-pity which is a mob-vice and the damning sloppiness — the real *trahison des clercs* — that certain intellectuals of our time passively cultivate. He recognizes that he is the active and responsible instrument as well as the victim of violence, and is prepared to do penance until such time as he receives absolution not from his own or from any human will, but, as a Greek might have said, from within the tragedy itself. To suppose that Valerie pardons Philip and that therefore he is freed from his guilt would be to miss the truth. Nor is Heron a source of pardon. Man does not absolve man, though man, on earth or in the spirit, may be a channel through which absolution flows.

5

Each of these characters asks his own question of the age of violence and asks it in his own way, and each seems from time to time to look at Heron, or to remember him, as though to read his answer. But Heron was not a man who would have pretended to answer for others. He may have been an impregnator in the sense that evidences of his life might or might not take root and flower in the lives of others — might or might not according to the need and nature of the soil upon which the seed fell. But he was not an instructor, a proponent of a system. He was not even a leader of men, except in the limited sense in which an efficient officer must be, and when Frewer showed a tendency to hero-worship, Heron at once made this clear. He was not a propagandist of his own way of life; he was 'quiet and included' in the age of violence — that was all; and that is why, in the setting of the Chassaignes' granary, he interested me.

He was, as I understand him, a man whose special quality was this: that, without withdrawal from the world or renouncement of its normal duties and affections,

he had reached a condition of interior equilibrium.
Many among us, hag-ridden by the anxieties and frustra-
tions of the world, fling themselves into rebellion against
it or drown themselves in self-pity; and some, in an
attempt to rationalize both self-pity and rebellion, have
adopted a philosophy of fragmentation which, from the
premise that all is vanity, even the will, even the soul,
argues the absolute discontinuity, and so the irre-
sponsibility, of human behaviour. This philosophy, by
denying any real distinction between violence and non-
violence, makes ready the way of violence. Subscribed
to by men of learning, it has its cant equivalent in the
phrase: 'It couldn't matter less'; in various forms, it is,
at the same time, an esoteric, a fashionable and a mob-
philosophy, and is cultivated by the agents of violence
as a useful cancer in the brain of the West. Heron, if he
had lived, would have been exempt from it and even
from fear of it. In his action he would have resisted it
as a man in health resists the onset of disease, but it
would have had no power over his inmost being. He
recognized the perversions of society and fought against
them, as a man defends his house against thieves, but he
did not live in an obsession of thieves. Looking in himself and in others for a peace within all wars and a sanity
within all madness, he was not torn by our anxieties.

This gift of quiet evident in him is not, I believe,
receivable by a few only, though few in the modern
world open themselves to it, and, when we encounter it
in a man, we are inclined to say: 'What is this quality
in him that is so unspectacular and yet gives him such
strength and serenity — that makes him so certainly a

man we should like to have with us in a tight corner and in the hour of death?' It has become unfamiliar, but is not therefore inaccessible.

It has become unfamiliar because, for half a century and longer, amid the world's preoccupation with collectivism, its value has been little taught. It has been confused with indifferentism, with escapism, with an absence of social conscience, and so has been taught *against* in many schools where education is thought of as vocational or as a political instrument, and in many pulpits whose emphasis has been on conduct.

Like all else that is good, like poetry and love, it is a grace — that is to say, a gift that is not a bargain and is infinitely available to all men without their deserving. But we must be in a state to receive it. We create nothing; we receive all things; even the phrase 'creative art' is a superficiality, for, as I once wrote elsewhere, 'all perfect art is a likeness of God carved by Himself in the sleep of the artist'. We receive in different kinds according to our natures, as streams flow in different beds and with varying abundance, though they arise from one source, and the mark of failure in us is aridity.

Power to receive the gift of interior quiet — or, as Kabir said, to be still amid all activities — is within the reach of the simplest among us as it is of the subtlest scholar. It seems to depend upon a power to make — or, I would say rather, to accept as axiomatic — certain distinctions, the breaking down of which is a crumbling of the banks that protect the stream from wastage; and this acceptance may be intuitive or intellectual or, as in Heron's case, both. We may cry out in wonder at the beauty of Michelangelo's Pietà, or we may know, or believe we know, why it is beautiful. In either case, if we are stilled by it, we have made a distinction that quiets the howling of the world, just as a French soldier of the earlier war made such a distinction when he observed, during an interval in the bombardment of his trench, that swallows were late that spring.

These saving distinctions — between, for example, man as a political animal and man as a spiritual being, between the virtue of a thing in itself and its utility or effect, between truth and opinion, between the just and the expedient — are precisely those distinctions that violence seeks to destroy, for they, and above all the mind that accepts them, are a distillation of the good that mankind has received from the Greek, the Roman, and the Christian civilizations, and from the great philosophies of the East. They are all comprised in the saying : 'The Kingdom of God is within you', and their difficulties are stated in another : 'Render therefore unto Caesar the things which are Caesar's ; and unto God the things that are God's'. But these sayings are so old that Western civilization had begun to mumble them and pass them by, over-confident that, in spite of all our sins and follies, the essential distinction made by them would be preserved. Never until our age of instantaneous communication, of mechanized power, of the penetration of violence into all men's thought, was an attempt made to expunge the distinction between God and Caesar from the *nature* of mankind. There have been wars and tyrants and little men who set themselves up as gods, and there have been slaves by arms and slaves by whip ;

but never before has it been claimed that all men are by nature slaves with no being but in Caesar, in the State, in the soulless anonymity of the mass. In face of this threat, which has imposed the age of violence upon us, it is natural and inevitable that men whose outward lives are torn by it should seek to preserve within them an interior life that is 'quiet and included'. Heron did no more and no less than this.

I do not see him as being outwardly exceptional; indeed it is a point that he was not. He was neither a saint nor a man of genius, nor, even potentially, the darling of a cult or a drawing-room. No freak, no rebel, no defier of custom for the sake of defiance, no claimant of exemption for himself from the common rule of courtesy and obligation, but a good officer who, playing no tricks with his conscience, assumed, as a matter of course, that, being made prisoner, it was his duty, when he could, to escape and fight. And it has been my experience that as, in the religious, vision may be sustained by ritual, so in the great Services it may be sustained by the very ordinariness of discipline. We are weak, our minds are naturally discursive, and it is of help to us, in cultivating our garden, that it should not all lie open to the four winds of our pride, but be sheltered in part by certain absolutes which we accept and whose service may become our freedom. This I take to have been true of Heron, and one of the reasons for what Philip Sturgess was tempted to call his 'indifferentism'. Heron was content to write a poem and use it as a spill, not because he did not value the poem but because he had learned to value nothing by its effect. It mattered nothing to him what, seemingly, he lost. 'Loss without losing. Why not? Isn't that a subject for poetry?' And when the poem was burnt unread and unremembered : 'It makes no difference what you keep. The thing was there before you had it, and is still there when it seems to have gone.'

Perhaps Heron's attitude may be summed up in this : that all other verbs are temporal, but the verb 'to be' is eternal ; or, more simply, by saying that he travelled light with no baggage that violence could take away. Least of all could his life be taken away, and the absolution of those who had seemed to take it was ever-present within the tragedy. They had only to learn how to receive it.

But if we ask how to live in the age of violence, certainly there is no answer that one man may give to another. Our hope of deliverance is in the asking, and in being aware that it is a spiritual and personal, and not an economic or collective, question that we ask. Mazzini's words of 1849 may give us a rule of conduct : 'We must act like men who have the enemy at their gates, and at the same time like men who are working for eternity'. But that is a rule of conduct only. Our questioning strikes deeper. We are asking, each for himself, how to reconjugate the verb 'to be' under the menace of those who would exclude it from the language of thought.

Siena
March 1952

CHARACTERS

(in order of appearance)

PHILIP STURGESS, *an American.* Age (in Acts I and III), 31 ; (in Act II), 27

COMMANDER JULIAN WYBURTON, R.N. (retired), age (in Acts I and III), 38 ; (in Act II), 34

MARIE CHASSAIGNE (Mrs. Wyburton), *a Frenchwoman.* Age (in Acts I and III), 31 ; (in Act II), 27

MRS. MURIVEN, *an old lady*

VALERIE BARTON, age (in Acts I and III), 26

MAJOR JOHN LANG (called HERON), age (in Act II), 29

DICK FREWER, age (in Act II), 21

PIERRE CHASSAIGNE, *an old Frenchman*

SCENES

Act I   Scene 1 : The garden of the Wyburtons' house in Gloucestershire
A Friday in July 1947.   Before dinner
2 : The same.   After dinner
Act II   Scene 1 : The granary of the Chassaignes' house at Blaise in the neighbourhood of Toulouse
July 1943.   11.50 P.M.
2 : The same.   Twelve days later.   Nearly 9.30 P.M.
3 : The same.   Three minutes to midnight
Act III   Scene 1 : As in Act I.   July 1947
The next morning, Saturday
2 : The same.   That evening

ACT I

ACT I

Scene 1

A quiet summer's evening, July 1947. Friday. A little before dinner. Full sunlight. A part of the lawn outside the drawing-room of the Wyburtons' house, called Stanning Farm, in Gloucestershire. It was formerly a Dower House. Period: early eighteenth century.

The lawn is part of a plateau or ledge, looking out over two converging valleys. We are looking South by East; a few small tree-tops appearing above our upstage horizon and a tranquil, open sky, which the sun will paint gradually, give an impression of falling ground. To the South-West (up-Right) is the beginning of a wood through the branches of which, if the electrician has adequate resources, the sun may appear gleamingly, and in the recesses of which, as time goes on, owls may, perhaps, profitably hoot.

On our Left is a part of the west end of the house, the main façade of which is invisible round our up-Left corner, for the house's 'aspect' is S.S.E. What we see is the end of the drawing-room. There are pleasant twelve-paned windows, through which, when necessary, light will shine out on to the lawn, and a door, now open on to the garden, with perhaps a pair of steps. This wall must be set far enough across to give us a glimpse of pictures and furniture and an active sense of there being a domestic interior.

The lawn can be as simple as the designer pleases. The essentials are: Near the house, to Left of Centre and two-thirds upstage, a table with garden chairs, a stool, and perhaps a lilo. These must appear to be 'inhabited'; books, papers, a sun-hat, a rug, are lying about. Farther downstage and to Right of Centre is an immovable seat, large enough for three, comfortable for two, preferably an eighteenth-century stone seat with a curving back. Its position is important. It is far enough from the table-group to separate (at any rate by convention) two conversations, but not so far as to give the impression that those who choose the stone seat are deliberately isolating themselves. It is easy to talk across the gap. Therefore the seat faces not straight downstage but N.N.E. Those who sit in it look out, clear of the line of the drawing-room wall, over a rolling countryside into the backward stage-box on the audience's Left, but if they glance over their right shoulders they take in the table-group.

When the Curtain rises, PHILIP STURGESS, *an American about thirty years old, an alive, cultivated, intelligent New Englander, who will sometimes use a Middle West accent to amuse his hosts, is seated near the table. He is wearing a dinner-jacket and pretending to look at a newspaper. But he is enjoying himself too much for newspapers. Letting the paper drop, he rises and wanders leisurely to look at the view, first upstage with his back to us, then facing us over the back of the stone seat.*

*   JULIAN WYBURTON, *a hard-bitten naval commander also in a dinner-jacket, comes in from the drawing-room with a silver cigarette box in his hand.*

4

JULIAN

(*Looking at* PHILIP *and in a mocking, affectionate tone*)
Silent upon a peak in Darien!

PHILIP

(*Rousing himself*)
I prefer Gloucestershire. These valleys take some
beating, though we have some in Maine.

JULIAN

You're down early. I shall have to desert you.
Tucker has a natural genius for ruining wine if you let
him touch it. I have left the sherry in the drawing-room.
Ladies may want it there. Help yourself when you feel
like it.

PHILIP

(*Grinning, and stretching himself luxuriously like a happy
schoolboy*)
I always have been early for exciting parties. I like
to sit and feel them coming.

JULIAN

(*Pleased and kindly*)
Is this to be such an exciting party?

PHILIP

For me it is — as you know. I can't be grateful
enough to you and Marie. I owed you plenty before
this, God knows. Now if things go well— (*This
seriousness is embarrassing to* JULIAN *and he turns it.*)

JULIAN

My dear Philip, Marie and I didn't create the young woman.

PHILIP

You invited her here the night I came.

JULIAN

Not for your sweet sake. We had never seen her in our lives before. She just happened to be staying with Mrs. Muriven.

PHILIP

I like the old lady too.

JULIAN

The Iron Duke? I wonder whether, as a hopeful idealist, you ought to like her. She doesn't mince her thoughts. . . . Take a drink when you want it. I'll go and carry up the rest. . . . Cigarettes in the box. Yours in fact. We live on what you brought from America. (*And he makes off.*)

PHILIP

(*Checking his exit*)

Julian!

JULIAN

What?

PHILIP

About what you call 'the young woman'. About Valerie Barton. Tell me. Do you think I'm a fool?

JULIAN

Why should I?

PHILIP

Maybe I am. Eight days isn't long. Still, I have to go back home. Valerie is going to South Africa, I gather. You see, Julian——

JULIAN

Now don't start reasoning it out. Your countrymen, I grant you, sometimes take a bit long in starting across the Atlantic but, when you do come, you don't waste time — in love or war. Eight days, eight hours, eight seconds — quite long enough to fall in love. Hence the word 'fall'.

PHILIP

Maybe she doesn't see it that way. . . . But certainly we have talked a lot.

JULIAN

No doubt you have. (*He is moving off into the draw-ing-room again, when he turns suddenly and asks in a hard, changed voice:*) What about? (PHILIP *looks up, startled by the question, and* JULIAN *repeats — an insistent staccato, separating his words*) What have you talked about?

PHILIP

What on earth do you mean? What should we talk about? Ourselves mostly. Her childhood in the North somewhere. She had a brother she likes to talk of. My childhood, too. (*Apologetically*) One does, you know. My home in Maine. My job as a teacher. The chance of a professorship at Harvard — a good outside chance anyway — which might mean——

7   c

JULIAN

Not about the River Line?

PHILIP

She knows of course that you and Marie and I met in occupied France. Not much more, surprisingly enough.

JULIAN

Why 'surprisingly'?

PHILIP

(*With easy good-humour*)

Well, I know I talk. I dare say you and Marie have found me a bit of an old soldier with my tales of battles long ago. But to Valerie, not much about war. Maybe she's had enough of it. It was two years longer for you British.

JULIAN

I shouldn't let that deter you. Othello used to charm Desdemona with talk of battles. Recognized technique.

PHILIP

Why so bitter, Julian?

JULIAN

I'm not. Just interested. It beats me why you *want* to talk of the River Line at all. Why do you?

PHILIP

That's a fair question. I'm not sure I know the answer. . . . Partly that I was responsible for what happened. . . . Or shall we say: One adventure in a calm scholastic life? The only time I've ever put my neck out. I'm sorry, I can't help it. For you and Marie it's different. You are professionals; I'm an amateur. You, as a naval officer first of all, and——

JULIAN

A much safer job than a schoolmaster's, I promise you. At least the Navy is not co-educational.

PHILIP

And a secret agent's? Are you going to pretend that's peaceful too?

JULIAN

Tediously celibate.

PHILIP

You laugh everything away. . . . Tell me, how many men — and women — have you seen killed, Julian? I mean, killed . . . privately, apart from battle? (*This is the kind of question* JULIAN *hates.*)

JULIAN

Good God, what a question! I've always been taught that it's rude to count.

PHILIP

Well, I have seen one.

JULIAN

And that makes you want to talk about it.

PHILIP

Does that surprise you?

JULIAN

Only that I can't imagine it in myself. I couldn't tell that story if I wanted to. (*He is speaking now with a steely restraint which is very like contempt, half-angry, half-mocking.*) When you tell 'the River Line Story' in America what on earth *do* you say?

PHILIP

Come, Julian, you're on edge. (*Rising*) Let me come down and help you carry up the wine.

JULIAN

There's time enough for that. I want to know how you begin.

PHILIP

(*Humouring him*)

You want me to do penance. Very well. What I say is this: Maybe, folks, you heard about the River Line? (*He is caricaturing himself now and using an exaggerated American accent.*) It was a set-up for helpin' our fliers get home when they'd been shot down. I was one of 'em. We were handed on from post to post, through Belgium, through France, into Spain — home that way. We were rafts towed down the River Line, you might say; or— (*No accent*) Isn't that harmless enough?

JULIAN

As far as it goes. I didn't know you could speak Chicago.

PHILIP

It isn't Chicago. It's pure tall corn out of Iowa.
Do I continue the performance?

JULIAN

Yes, please. It's the end that matters.

PHILIP

(*The exaggerated accent again*)
Well, boys, as I was tellin' you, on the way south—
it was the last lap before the Spanish frontier——

JULIAN

Do you give the names of the places?

PHILIP

(*No accent*)
I have said Blaise.

JULIAN

Blaise is no matter. Marie was captured. She's
hopelessly compromised. She could never go back
anyhow.

PHILIP

Go back! Do you . . . the war's over, Julian.

JULIAN

Wars crop up, you know. . . . Well, go on. You
were saying: 'It was the last lap before the Spanish
frontier'. What do you say then?

PHILIP

Julian, what *is* this?

JULIAN

I want to know what *you* say.

PHILIP

(*Sharply, for he is being sorely tried.   No accent now.
Very fast*)

I say : Marie was in charge of us.   We lay up in her father's house.   Three of us at first — a boy called Dick ; a fellow with long thin legs we nicknamed Heron, and myself.   One night, Marie brought in another Britisher, Julian——

JULIAN

Or Wyburton?

PHILIP

Julian.

JULIAN

Are you sure of that?

PHILIP

I think of you that way.   I've always called you that way.   Dead sure.

JULIAN

Good.   Not that it really matters.   My cat is out of the bag.

PHILIP

Now can I come out of the corner?   (JULIAN, *for a
moment, grasps his arm, then lets it go.*)   You know, Julian, if I do tell that story — or try to . . . (*Then he begins again.*)   The facts, yes, but they don't mean any-thing apart from the extraordinary peace of that damned comfortless granary.   And Heron, right up to the end, was the heart of it.   I still have the feel of that — our

group of five, bound together then and bound together still. Not only we three survivors but all five, the dead and the living, still bound together in spite of what happened——

JULIAN

Or because of it.

PHILIP

But you hate to speak of it.

JULIAN

Of the River Line? I don't hate to speak of it with you. But it's hard to speak of it without speaking of Heron, and in this house——

PHILIP

Isn't it best to speak of him quite simply and openly? What was done had to be done. (JULIAN *looks into his face and says nothing. Then:*)

JULIAN

I never speak of him to Marie or she to me. . . . No doubt you'll tell me that is wrong psychologically. But I tell you it is necessary.

PHILIP

Because — I can say this to you, Julian — because at that time she loved Heron? (*This is true and* JULIAN *knows it, but it is so far from being his reason for not speaking of* HERON *to his wife that he is, for a moment, taken aback. Then he accepts it.*)

13

JULIAN

That reason will do as well as another.

PHILIP

But it is true.

JULIAN

Oh yes, it's true enough. (*They are side by side, looking out over the valley, their backs to the drawing-room in the open door of which* MARIE *now appears. She is in a simple evening dress, carrying a tray with decanter and glasses.*)

MARIE

You are very silent.

JULIAN
(*Turning*)

You dressed? What time is it?

MARIE

They may be here in a few minutes. The Iron Duke is dangerously punctual.

JULIAN

I still have the wine to do.

MARIE

Good heavens, but it will be ruined! At this hour — Musigny!

JULIAN

It was decanted long ago. It only needs carrying up.

14

MARIE

Well, my darling. . . . (*Meaning: 'Well, for heaven's sake, fetch it!'*)

JULIAN

Take warning, Philip. Never marry a Frenchwoman. They have a taste in wine. Even your cellar isn't your own. (*Exit.*)

MARIE

(*Pouring out sherry*)

No cocktails. Better keep to the grape when it's good. Is that all right?

PHILIP

Perfect. (*He sits beside her.*)

MARIE

Happy?

PHILIP

Very.

MARIE

On a summer's evening, looking down that valley — this must be a good place to be happy in.

PHILIP

Must be? Aren't you happy too?

MARIE

In some ways I am. Did you doubt it?

PHILIP

I confess I did before I came.

15

MARIE

(*With a candid non-egotism that is part of her character*)

It surprises me a little that in America you should have troubled your head about me.

PHILIP

But, Marie, it stands to reason I'm grateful——

MARIE

No, my dear, don't say what you were going to say. Blaise was . . . a Service incident like another.

PHILIP

Ah, you and Julian, the French and the English of your kind, you take a professional and Service view of everything.

MARIE

Is that wrong?

PHILIP

Well, I believe it's limiting. The world has to think in terms of peace or it won't have peace. Sometimes I feel with you and Julian as if you felt that the war was still going on. And so you won't talk about it. You behave as if heroism were not heroism, as if feeling were not felt. (*She flinches in protest.*) Oh, I know you *do* feel, all right. But you won't ever acknowledge it. You clip yourselves into your professional reticences as if they were a suit of armour that won't let you breathe——

MARIE

(*With emphasis*)

Or go limp.

16

PHILIP

But why can't you relax? Isn't it an affectation not to?

MARIE

(*With a shrug*)

A habit. A valuable one, perhaps, never, as Julian says, 'to spill over'. Aren't there enough people spilling enthusiasm and grievances in this world? . . . No, Philip, I see your point. But don't forget that at Blaise I was the postman and you were the parcels. You will agree that it is desirable for a postman to train himself to think impersonally of his parcels. . . . As you know, I didn't always succeed.

PHILIP

You mean Heron? . . . Tell me, Marie, straight out now; you would rather I didn't speak of him?

MARIE

(*With difficulty*)

I would rather you didn't when Julian is here. . . . But now you and I are alone, and Julian needn't be . . . wounded — yes, it would be a relief, from silence, to hear you speak of him to me. Don't think, dear Philip, that there is . . . anything wrong with my marriage — except certain silences. Julian and I love each other with all our hearts — across the silence. Heron is long dead. Is it four years? . . . And when one whom we have loved, however silently, is dead, all account of him from those who were with him when we were not is precious, seeming — oh, I am French. How would you say that

17

in English? I say it so stiffly . . . seeming to extend his life in our memory which cannot now be extended in our experience.

PHILIP

I dream of Heron often, particularly since I've been your guest in this house.

MARIE

This house is full of him.

PHILIP

Dream and memory get mixed up. In the morning I'm never sure which is which. Last night in my dream I was back in a little dark room in Brussels where Heron and Frewer and I were first brought together — where, so to speak, the River Line began. The little grey man in charge there was cross-examining us and explaining and explaining how careful he had to be. He was terrified that a German agent might introduce himself into the line and be forwarded down it from stage to stage and then mop up the *whole* Line. In fact, he explained this to us quite calmly, but in my dream he was wild with terror. He kept on saying 'un faux Anglais, a sham Englishman, a sham Englishman, a sham Englishman — that is what we have most to fear', and in my dream, as he said this, he kept on looking at Heron——

MARIE
(*In agony, stopping him*)
Ah, Philip, Philip — no.

18

PHILIP

But I must tell you this, because whenever I dream of Heron it's always the same. I looked across the table at Heron and what I saw wasn't just his appearance but the essential character of him : not just his tallness and erectness and his way of carrying himself that made us call him Heron, but a kind of *movement* upward so that, in some extraordinary way, you felt that he was, physically . . . light?

MARIE

(*Primly because she is deeply moved*)

That is exact. Light. Not burdened. Not tethered. Light. That is . . . exact.

PHILIP

I believe it was that more than anything else which made Frewer and me . . . love him the way we did. Certainly it was that which prevented me from putting two and two together about him. I ought to have known. All along the line before we came to your place there were indications. He took French stamps out of a desk, and once he bought French stamps. What could a genuine Englishman want with French stamps? There was the incident with the German corporal. There were lots and lots of little things. Above all that he spoke the German of a German, and, for Frewer's benefit and mine, made a kind of comedy out of the way he led them up the garden path.

MARIE

Was it the fact of his being so proud of his German that first made you suspect him? Wasn't his German

19

the very thing that, as an enemy agent, he would have soft-pedalled?

PHILIP

Not necessarily. Not on the principle of a double-bluff. . . . But, Marie, I didn't suspect him until the last moment. You must understand that. I dare say I ought to have. The indications were all there. I dare say I was hopelessly guileless or 'unprofessional' if you like, but it's true : all the way from Brussels to Blaise, and for all the time we spent in your granary, I didn't suspect him. If I had, I should have found a way to tell you and Julian sooner. . . .

MARIE

But why are you defending yourself? I'm not blaming you, God knows.

PHILIP

But you think I was unprofessional. (MARIE *makes a little helpless gesture at this misunderstanding.*) You must understand. In spite of all the indications I didn't *consciously* suspect. To me it simply wasn't credible that Heron was false. I loved talking to him. I loved being with him. I was thinking all the time of the personal relationship. I let all the indications go — there they were, but I let them go, until, at the very end, they rushed together and . . . became . . . certainty. You see, Marie——

MARIE

Philip, please, please get it out of your head that I

am blaming you. It's all over. I'm not even accusing
you of professional neglect.

PHILIP

What then, Marie? Something — not Heron's death
only, but something else is troubling you. (JULIAN
appears.)
What is it?

MARIE
(*Seeing* JULIAN)
Is everything set?   The wine, I mean?

JULIAN

You speak as if a dinner-party were a military operation. I suppose it is to the French. The ammunition
is beside the gun. (*He looks out upstage.*) There are
our guests.

MARIE

On foot?

JULIAN

Half way across the field. (PHILIP *too looks out
eagerly.*)   You'd better go and meet them, Philip.

PHILIP

I doubt that.

JULIAN
(*His arm on* MARIE'S *shoulder*)
Why are you on edge? You've been talking too
much or listening too much.

21

MARIE

I shall be all right. . . . I get tired, quite suddenly, but it goes. (*She sits.*) Oh I wish that part of my pleasure in every pleasant thing — in just sitting here and being peaceful — weren't the negative joy of its not being hell. (*She reaches for* JULIAN's *hand.*) You and I shall have that all our lives. To live with the feeling that happiness is exceptional — something momentarily allowed. That's the difference between you and us, Philip. That's the answer to your question: 'why not relax?' We have lived all our lives on a campaign or between campaigns. All Europeans of our age have and — Sorry, Julian.

JULIAN

Meanwhile we farm our land, my dear.

MARIE

Yes — but 'meanwhile' . . . No, I'm sorry. Take no notice of me. Go and meet them, Philip.

PHILIP

Take it easy, Marie. (*Begins to go.*)

JULIAN
(*Steadying her*)

'For, if thou rest not, busy maggots eat thy brain, and all is dedicate to chaos.'

PHILIP
(*Turning*)

Who wrote that?

22

JULIAN

That? Oh, it applies to all of us, not to Marie only: to the hopeful idealists as well. 'O proud, impatient Man——' You know it?

'O proud, impatient Man, allow to Earth
Her seasons.   Growth and change require their winter
As a tired child his sleep.   Thou art that child;
Lie down.   This is the night.   Day follows soon.
Wake then refreshed, wiser for having slept.
This is old nurses' counsel, and the gods',
For, if thou rest not, busy maggots eat
Thy brain, and all is dedicate to chaos.'

MARIE

That, I suppose, is what Heron meant by 'a creative pause'.

PHILIP

I thought you were a naval officer.   How do you memorize these things?   That ought to be my job.

JULIAN

Oh, we got leave you know. . . . Besides, memory is my vice.   In my job, one doesn't carry things in writing. (PHILIP *goes.   They are silent until he is gone.*)

JULIAN

Was he talking of Heron?

MARIE

I let him. . . . It's you I love, Julian.

JULIAN
Yes, my darling, I know.   (*A distant knock is heard.*)

MARIE
(*Rising*)
They are at the front door.

JULIAN
Yes.   Stay here peacefully until they come.   Philip
will bring them through.   (*The knock is repeated.*)

MARIE
I hate the sound of knocking at the door.   (*She links
her arm in his and holds it closely.*)

Curtain

ACT I

SCENE 2

The same, after dinner. On the table is an unlighted lamp. As it is summer-time, there is plenty of daylight left, but the producer can do what he likes with the sunset as time passes. When the Curtain rises the stage is empty and the windows are dark. But the drawing-room lights are soon switched on. Movement is visible inside and women's voices are heard. Enter from the drawing-room MARIE, *followed by* MRS. MURIVEN *and* VALERIE.

MARIE

I don't think we should be cold out here. But you decide, Mrs. Muriven, please.

MRS. MURIVEN

I wouldn't dream of sitting anywhere else. It is an enchanting evening. I have arranged with the sun not to set at present. To sit out after dinner in England is an extremely rare luxury. Let us indulge in it until it is taken from us.

VALERIE

It isn't one that any Government is likely to take away.

MRS. MURIVEN

I am not sure, Valerie. Nature is by no means egalitarian; the sun often shines on the Riviera when there is a fog in Merthyr Tydfil. That cannot be described as social justice.

MARIE

If you are comfortable and will forgive me, I will go and fetch coffee.

VALERIE

Let me help.

MARIE

No, please. It is a secret ritual.

MRS. MURIVEN

(*Cheerfully grumpy*)

Why do you and Julian do so much of your servants' work?

MARIE

We do it so much better. (*Exit.*)

VALERIE

Godmother, how could you ask that?

MRS. MURIVEN

I? Oh, I can ask anything. I knew Julian's mother before he was born. I must be allowed to poke fun at his wife. But how she can cook! . . . I like your American, my dear.

VALERIE

Mine?

MRS. MURIVEN

That was the word I used.

VALERIE

I thought he talked well at dinner.

26

MRS. MURIVEN

I found that he listened well. A gift I appreciate more. . . . Still, I should like to have drawn him about the River Line.

VALERIE

Some of that I *have* heard.

MRS. MURIVEN

I got only bits and pieces.

VALERIE

He puts them together like a jig-saw puzzle — as if he weren't sure of the answer himself.

MRS. MURIVEN

Julian and Marie don't give him much chance on that subject.

VALERIE

Oh? . . . Why do you say that?

MRS. MURIVEN

Twice at dinner, they — in effect — stopped him. The first time, Julian switched the conversation away; the second time, Marie rose from table and swept out, taking poor Mr. Sturgess's audience with her. It seemed odd to me. I was enjoying my pear.

VALERIE

Why should it be 'odd'? Isn't it only that they don't want to talk of war?

27

MRS. MURIVEN

I may be wrong, though that, in the nature of things, is improbable. But the two of them always refuse at the same fence. Has Mr. Sturgess talked to you of the man they called Heron?

VALERIE

A little. He often begins to talk about him. He seems to want to. Then he stops.

MRS. MURIVEN

Why does he stop — even to you?

VALERIE

I believe he's not sure of his own story.

MRS. MURIVEN

But he was there!

VALERIE

Oh yes, he was there.

MRS. MURIVEN

Julian and Marie are sure enough. But I repeat: they always refuse at the same fence.

VALERIE

How you love a mystery!

MRS. MURIVEN

On the contrary, it is precisely what I don't love. If I am suddenly whisked away from the dinner-table

28

before I have finished my dessert, I like to know, quite clearly, why.

VALERIE

(*After a pause and a movement, during which* MARIE *appears with the coffee tray*)

You never will, dear Godmother, until you have solved the mystery of sudden death. (MARIE *stands quite still.* VALERIE *sees her.*) I'm sorry. I suppose that doesn't make sense. I had jumped off down a side-track from something Godmother was saying. I mean : one supposes that certain things won't happen to oneself. Even those that must happen. We have an idea that *we* are exempt. Even from death. It's against reason that we should be, but I believe that in our heart of hearts we are all incredulous.

MARIE

(*Very low but very distinctly and meditatively*)
Incredulous?

VALERIE

— of death, seen in the distance.

MARIE

Why only 'in the distance'?

VALERIE

Isn't it so?

MARIE

But not only so. Not 'in the distance' only. Seen close. Seen close. Why not? That is the very word — incredulous ! (*She is seeing the face of* HERON *as he died. Now, swiftly pulling herself together, she puts down the*

29

tray.) Coffee? . . . (*To* VALERIE) I'm sorry. I interrupted you. I too — what did you say? — leap down
a side-track and then shout at innocent people who
can't have been expected to follow. I do beg your
pardon . . . (*To* MRS. MURIVEN) Black or white?

MRS. MURIVEN

Black, please.

VALERIE

(*In answer to a glance*)
And for me. (PHILIP *arrives. While he is being given
coffee*—)

MRS. MURIVEN

I hope the gentlemen enjoyed their port?

MARIE

Is Julian on his way?

VALERIE

(*Who has wandered upstage and has been looking out
over the countryside and is now returned*)
This must be one of the pleasantest views in England,
whichever way you look. It's like being in a huge armchair looking over the two valleys. (*To* MRS. MURIVEN)
I'm glad you have told the sun not to set.

PHILIP

You said that in a very melancholy way.

VALERIE

Did I? This is one of my last evenings in England.

PHILIP

But your passage hasn't come through?

VALERIE

It may at any moment now.

PHILIP

You aren't looking forward to South Africa.

VALERIE

In a way, I am. My brother needs me there. Anyhow I look forward to the voyage. The trouble is that nowadays no voyage is long enough. What I should really like is to go round the world in a sailing-ship — no newspaper, no wireless, a little plain company — not too much — and all the books I want to read again.

PHILIP

Again? No new books?

VALERIE

Those as well, I suppose.

PHILIP

And what did you mean by *plain* company?

VALERIE

Seamen, doctors, soldiers — people getting on with their own jobs — does that seem dull?

PHILIP

Not if it includes schoolmasters.

31

VALERIE

By no means all!

PHILIP

One would do. Where do I find a sailing-ship?

MARIE

Dear Philip, what on earth are you talking about?

MRS. MURIVEN

I think he was planning to elope with my god-daughter in a seven-masted schooner.

PHILIP

I hope you approve?

MRS. MURIVEN

I approve the schooner. I must have notice of the other part of the question. (JULIAN *appears with bottles of liqueurs and cognac, and* MARIE'S *coat over his arm.*)

JULIAN

Marie, take one of these rather quickly. (*She moves to him.*)

PHILIP
(*To* VALERIE)

Anyhow, I made you forget that you were going to South Africa.

JULIAN
(*To* MARIE)

No, the one under my arm.

VALERIE
(*To* PHILIP)

Yes, you did.

PHILIP

Q.E.F. Which was to be done. (*While the others make room on the table for* JULIAN'S *bottles,* PHILIP *seats himself beside* VALERIE *on the stone seat.*

PHILIP

Tell me about your brother.

VALERIE

In South Africa?

PHILIP

No. The other one.

VALERIE

He was killed. I have told you.

PHILIP

Not enough.

VALERIE

He was my half-brother really. They both were. But he counted as a real brother.

(*From the group at the table.*)

MRS. MURIVEN

No, Julian, bless you, not cognac.

JULIAN

It's Delamain Oh Six.

MRS. MURIVEN

Even so.

JULIAN

I thought it was your favourite tipple.

MRS. MURIVEN

But it makes my heart beat.

(*From the stone seat.*)

VALERIE

Even Godmother is growing old. She has changed since I saw her. But that was in the weeks before Dunkirk. One always forgets how long the war went on.

PHILIP

Why didn't you meet Julian then?

VALERIE

Commander Wyburton? But I have never been *here* until now. Godmother didn't live here then. It was in Yorkshire, in the house she had shared with my Grandmamma — who was German. Does that surprise you?

PHILIP

You mean does it shock me? Why should it? You forget I'm American. We aren't all Pilgrim Fathers.

VALERIE

But you know, I'm really more German than one grandmother accounts for. Her family came out of Germany in the sixties and she clung to the old world and rubbed it into us. She and Godmother used to talk

34

German continually; so did our own mother; so did we. It's just as much my first language as English. Useful when war came.

PHILIP

In Yorkshire still?

VALERIE

In London. We had come south long before then. Grandmamma and my own mother had died and what with schools and jobs and growing up we didn't often go north. So we rather lost touch with Godmother. But my brother and I did go to see her during his last leave before going to France. Then the war flared up. It was the last time I saw her until now — and the last time I saw him. Of course he was older than me, but when I was small and even now. . . . However, that is of no interest except to me. For everyone else, he's dead.

PHILIP

But for you — not?

VALERIE

Never, really, while I myself am alive.

PHILIP

Which means?

VALERIE

He was everything. As if we were one. And he still is. (JULIAN *has come over and is standing beside her to offer her cognac, a glass in one hand, a bottle in the other. She looks at him, then away, and is not interrupted.*) Do you know what I mean if I say that we had each other's legends?

JULIAN

I do. (*They turn to him, a little resenting his interruption at first, then with interest.*) If you watch a child playing his own secret game, perhaps all you see is that he crawls backwards and forwards again and again over the same bit of grass, and touches the same stone as he passes, or turns it over, or looks at it in some special way. That stone may be Open Sesame for him or Mount Everest or a mouse. Anyhow he is performing his legend, and you are outside it and he is inside. . . . It's just the same later. Everyone builds a legend into his life which is — well, what is it?

VALERIE

The glow inside quite ordinary things?

JULIAN

Perhaps. . . . Anyhow, to be inside someone else's legend is . . . only once in all my life have I known a *man* capable of it.

VALERIE

Who? (*But* JULIAN *has turned abruptly away, and she continues to* PHILIP) My brother was in mine ; I was in his. I used to feel often that he was I, and I was he. I do still. I believe twins feel that sometimes. And he was only my half-brother and years older.

PHILIP

How was he killed?

VALERIE

(*Shaking a puzzled head*)

He was taken prisoner. He escaped. He must have been killed escaping. Anyhow he has never come home.

PHILIP

Is that really why you are going to South Africa? Must you?

VALERIE

It's no good staying here. He and I were going to live and work together after the war. So we planned.

PHILIP

Suppose one of you had married? Wasn't that a possibility?

VALERIE

I suppose so. We should have talked the same language about that, I expect. I don't know. I wasn't eighteen. (VALERIE *gets up and joins the other group.* PHILIP, *after a moment, wanders downstage, lights a cigarette, and rejoins her. Meanwhile,* MRS. MURIVEN, *continuing a conversation we have not heard, says:*)

MRS. MURIVEN

I'm not at all sure, Julian, that you are the right person for this discussion.

JULIAN

Because I agree too much?

MRS. MURIVEN

As a naval officer, responsibility is a profession with you. (*Seeing* PHILIP'S *approach*) Mr. Sturgess will be more profitable to quarrel with. . . . Come and sit down, Mr. Sturgess. Let us call in the New World to redress the indecisiveness of the Old.

PHILIP

What have I done?

MARIE

Mrs. Muriven believes that the Western democracies are dying of a sick conscience. No sooner have they acted than they regret it and draw back.

PHILIP

A little self-criticism may be no bad thing.

MRS. MURIVEN

Never cry over spilt decisions.

JULIAN

Certainly the Iron Duke never did!

VALERIE

It's quite useless to pull Godmother's leg about the Iron Duke. It's a nickname she adores.

MRS. MURIVEN

Do you wonder?

PHILIP

I do a little.

MRS. MURIVEN

Wasn't he a great man?

PHILIP

But he lived a long time ago — before democracy began.

MRS. MURIVEN

You forget how often, in the history of the world, democracy had failed before he was born. The epitaph is always the same : ' Here lies democracy who died of a sick conscience'. The funeral is attended by two pall-bearers. Their names are 'On the one hand' and 'On the other'. And on the tombstone is always written: 'He wanted too much too soon ; he paid too little too late'. . . . In America you learn fast. That is your genius. Fast enough, I believe — just fast enough — to save mankind. The world moves. You with it — inevitably.

PHILIP

May I ask in what direction?

MRS. MURIVEN

I am an old Englishwoman, Mr. Sturgess, but I have American blood. I love and respect your people. May I really try to answer that? In what direction?

PHILIP

Why, please! This is off the record.

MRS. MURIVEN

Why, then, in the direction of responsibility. Which doesn't mean counting appetites and calling them pro-gress or counting voices and calling them the voice of God. It means responsibility *within your destiny*. Like a pilot's responsibility for his ship, moving on a tide.

PHILIP

I like to believe in free will. 'Destiny' is a tough word for me.

MRS. MURIVEN

It is implied in history; it is implied in character; both tough customers if we want to please ourselves. You have become — forgive the word, there is no other — you have become a great imperial nation. Destiny sent your people westward across the Atlantic for three centuries and more, whether they liked it or not, and now it is drawing them back again. It drew *you* back. Do you imagine that you went bombing Germany because you wanted to?

PHILIP

Indeed I don't. . . . But Mrs. Muriven, you are driving mankind into an intolerable dilemma. It's Hamlet's dilemma between a violent action required of him by — oh, by Destiny if you like, and the peaceful quietism that was part of his nature. It tears the conscience. The Western democracies wish to avoid that tearing.

MRS. MURIVEN

Wish? Wish to avoid? . . . Responsibility is a hard bread to be eaten with a rough wine, not sopped in milk. No one can eat it for us. Eat or starve.

PHILIP

You don't leave much room for the people's will.

MRS. MURIVEN

Oh yes I do. 'Take what you want', said God.

'Take it, and pay for it.' But, having paid, don't ask for your money back.

MARIE

It is true. It is quite, quite true. Our responsibilities within our destiny select us, not we them ; they select us — often quite suddenly. It is like walking into a room that you expect to be empty, and finding a man there waiting for you and looking at you and commanding you. Always you recognize him, but sometimes at first you call him by the wrong name.

JULIAN
(*To divert her, with great abruptness*)
You are shivering, my dear. Look, I brought out your coat. Put it on.

MARIE

I am not cold, thank you.

JULIAN

Shall I light the lamp? It will soon be dark? (*He lights it but keeps it low.*)

MRS. MURIVEN

Suppose we were to stroll round the garden. It is the perfect time when the light is not all gone and the evening primroses are out.

PHILIP

A time to remember absent friends. (MRS. MURIVEN and JULIAN *move away upstage, and pause with their backs to us, looking down over garden and valley.* MARIE *has*

followed, but remains detached from them at two yards'
distance. From within the house comes the sound of piano
music, at first scarcely audible, then clear, then disappearing
— a very brief passage of the Scherzo of Chopin's Sonata
in B flat minor. At the first sound of it:)

VALERIE

Listen !

(*When the music ceases —*)

MARIE

What did you hear ?

VALERIE

I thought . . . music ?

MARIE

There's no one in the drawing-room.

VALERIE

One imagines things, I suppose.

MARIE

Did you know it ?

VALERIE

It was the Chopin Scherzo which is followed by . . .
I have known it all my life.

MARIE

What is it followed by ?

VALERIE

The Funeral March. (MARIE *turns and follows the others who have disappeared.*)

VALERIE

(*To* MARIE, *retreating*)

But you . . . (*To* PHILIP) Why should she pretend not to hear it?

PHILIP

I think she didn't.

VALERIE

Nor you? Do you mean that I alone — ? Do you mean that——

PHILIP

I heard it.

VALERIE

Not the others? You and I? . . . My brother played it. It is the B Flat Minor Sonata. I have always known it.

PHILIP

You were thinking of your brother. His death doesn't tear you?

VALERIE

No. Do you remember that story you began to tell at dinner? About your friend — I mean Heron — how one night he wrote a poem and, because it was your rule not to carry anything written, burnt it; and how he said it made no difference whether you kept a poem or not or whether anyone ever read it or not. The thing — any spiritual thing, I suppose — was there before you had it and is still there when it seems to have gone. My

43

brother taught me that. 'Loss without losing' was what you said.

PHILIP

It wasn't I who said it. It was Heron.

VALERIE

My brother didn't use those words, but it's what he felt and what I feel. That, you see, is why his death doesn't tear me.

PHILIP

The things I struggle after, you reach out for as if they belonged to you.

VALERIE

What things?

PHILIP

That music perhaps.

VALERIE

But you heard it too!

PHILIP

I thought so. If I did, it was through you. And now I begin to doubt it. It's always like that with me. . . . Oh I haven't the gift of . . . making confessions . . . flippantly. Perhaps with you I needn't try?

VALERIE
(*Gently*)

No, you needn't try.

PHILIP

(*Swerving to an opportunity*)

Why? Why on earth do you make special conditions for me?

VALERIE

Because I . . . Because you are exciting.

PHILIP

Good heavens, in what way?

VALERIE

You swerve suddenly. You . . . teach suddenly. (*Laughing at him*) Are you a good schoolmaster?

PHILIP

I doubt it. I don't teach myself suddenly enough. I suppose what I'm struggling for is some kind of reasoned balance between the activities and the acceptances of life — the crusading part and the quietist part of me, if you see what I mean.

VALERIE

But why not?

PHILIP

Because, like the rest of the world, I want it both ways. It's not enough for me to hear music ; I want to be quite sure I heard it and know why. But you — you did when you were speaking about Heron's poem — you speak of that balance between the two aspects of life — the active part and the accepting part — well, it's damned hard to say. You speak of it hardly at all as a *reasoned* thing. Much more as a thing to be felt, an experience within reach.

VALERIE

Not within my reach.   Reachable if you like.

PHILIP

Very well.   But in sight, like an apple on a high branch.   Heron's attitude towards his poem seemed to me, when Frewer told me of it, anyhow to a bit of me, a kind of . . . indifferentism?

VALERIE

But why?   To write a poem that no one will ever see and to care passionately about it — I understand that so well.   It's like fighting in a part of the battlefield that no one will ever notice, or loving, not for what love takes or even for what it gives. . . . Philip, that's not indifferentism.   Why do you think it can be?   It's not avoiding the fire or fearing it.   It is passing through the burning, fiery furnace without the smell of fire on you. I don't know any other way to live in the modern world. I think your friend . . . What was he?   I mean, by temperament?   Did he take a hopeful view of the world?

PHILIP

He took a much blacker view of what was going to *happen* than I did, if that is what you mean, but it didn't frighten him.

VALERIE

(*To herself*)

Making himself eyes with which to see in the dark.

46

PHILIP

Tell me something. It's rather a naïve question. Your godmother says I'm naïve.

VALERIE

What is it?

PHILIP

Are you Christian?

VALERIE

Yes. . . . I like your questions. They are sudden too.

PHILIP

I like your answers. Few people wouldn't hedge that answer. . . . Anyhow, you see, I have to risk being thought not subtle enough. I have to take short-cuts. I haven't long to get to know you. When you answer 'yes' like that, it's a long stride between you and me.

VALERIE

Did you love him — your friend, I mean?

PHILIP

Yes.

VALERIE

That — Oh, the thing's unsayable!

PHILIP

(*Near her*)

What were you trying to say?

47

VALERIE

Your 'yes', too, seemed a long stride between you and me. Does that make any kind of sense about a man I never knew?

PHILIP

It makes sense to me, knowing him and knowing you. Beginning to know you both.

VALERIE

It will soon be quite dark. I must go home.

PHILIP

They will come back.

VALERIE

I think they've gone on by the lower gate. . . . Philip, when your friend died——

PHILIP

Go on, my dear. Say it. You will say it straighter than I can.

VALERIE

I have no right to say it.

PHILIP

You have the right, if you will take it.

VALERIE

I meant that your conscience *is* torn by Heron's death. Do you know how your face changes when you speak of it or when you so terribly avoid speaking of it? . . . Oh, you don't know how your whole being seems to change. It's agony to watch.

PHILIP

Everything has altered since I came here. My romantic selection from the past doesn't work any more. The thing comes up and lives itself; to be with Marie and Julian is to have the stress and the ache of it; but you——

VALERIE

What have I to do with that story?

PHILIP

More than I can tell. You seem almost to be part of it, as though he really were still alive and I could stretch out my hand and take his . . . as I take yours. (*She makes no movement of withdrawal.*) Don't take your hand away.

VALERIE

No.

PHILIP

Never?

VALERIE

My dear, don't ask that now.

PHILIP

I do ask it.

VALERIE

Not to-night.

PHILIP

I do ask it.

VALERIE

Because to-night you are what he used to call 'out of judgement', and so, perhaps, am I. (*Their hands part.*)

PHILIP

Then you must hear the whole story first.

VALERIE

Why are you afraid of your story? Or didn't you know until now that you were?

PHILIP

I don't think I am. I don't think I am. I may not force it on Julian and Marie; they know it too well. . . . But I can tell it to you. You have the right. When you have heard it, you can . . . take your hand away —or not. (*They are now upstage.*)

VALERIE

Tell it as we walk home. . . . Philip, do you really want to tell me this? Better sleep on it and decide in the morning.

PHILIP

I want you to know . . . and judge.

VALERIE

Tell it then as you see it, but without judging yourself. How do you know that judgement lies with us?

PHILIP

We had better not leave the lamp.

VALERIE

There's no wind.

PHILIP

Safer to turn it out. (*He turns it out. She waits, then moves on as he comes up with her.*) Listen. You know already how we came to Marie's house. When we had been in her granary a week, she told us there was another Englishman coming. That night she went to bring him in and we sat up waiting. . . . (*They are gone now. There is still light in the sky and light flows out from the drawing-room windows.*)

Curtain

ACT II

ACT II

Scene 1

July 1943. Time: 11.50 P.M. The granary at the Chassaignes', near Blaise, in the neighbourhood of Toulouse. Three-quarters of the stage-width from the audience's Right is occupied by a room interior to the granary, called the Sardine Box. The remaining quarter of the stage has in the foreground a trap-door leading down to PIERRE CHAS-SAIGNE'S *room. Beyond this is dimly visible a background which suggests a huge granary piled with miscellaneous junk. This granary has been long diverted from its original purpose and has since been used as a vast boxroom and store; also as a playroom by* MARIE *when she was a young girl.*

There will be action downstage by the trap-door and in the Sardine Box but none in the further recesses of the granary, which are suggested by a distant skylight, plainly visible as you look across the trap-door and visible also above the walls of the Sardine Box, which are wooden partition walls and do not reach to the granary's sloping roof.

The Sardine Box should be small. It has four visible walls. On the Right, the wall is part of the main outside wall of the granary. It is almost entirely occupied by a very large granary door through which, if it were ever opened (which it is not), hay, etc., could be hoisted from an outside platform. Neither this platform nor the ladder which runs down from it to the ground is ever seen by the audience.

This granary door is fastened by a great bar (never used). In the granary door is a small door fastened by a wooden latch. As no part of the granary door, except this latch, moves during the play, it is not a carpenter's but a painter's job.

There are three other walls of the Sardine Box, all partitions. The first juts out above the granary door and runs parallel to the footlights to a little short of midstage — let us say from East to West, supposing the audience to be looking North. The second, a short wall, runs W.S.W. far enough to contain a door. The third runs a little West of South, almost straight at the footlights, which it would reach just to the East of the trap-door if it were not conventionally cut off in order not to interrupt the audience's line of sight. At the point where this wall is cut off, a stove-pipe runs up from the room below.

This inner room or Sardine Box is the place which is ordinarily used by the officers. Except at the trap-door itself on one or two occasions, the whole action passes in the Box. The officers do, in fact, sleep and often by day sit in the other parts of the granary, but we do not see them there. As their whole object is so to arrange things that, if they have to make a lightning get-away, they leave behind them nothing that could lead Germans to believe that the granary had been inhabited, the Sardine Box is a tangle of boxes and odd bits of furniture completely untidy and haphazard. There are a rug and an armchair on three legs, and there is as much else as the producer likes.

Over the skylight a blind has been fitted. At night this is pulled down and all those parts of the granary which lie outside the Sardine Box are blacked out, but the efficiency *of the black-out is distrusted and lamps are used only in the Sardine Box, not because the blind of the skylight is insufficient but because, outside the Sardine Box, there may be wall-chinks.*

Therefore the only artificial light outside the Sardine Box is one fixed and sheltered lamp (which the audience does not see) throwing an inward beam at floor-level which the audience does see, gleaming behind the trap-door. In the Sardine Box lamps can be safely moved but the tops of them are shaded so that they may not throw an upward light above the partition walls.

Before darkness falls (that is, in Scene 2), the blind is up and daylight penetrates from the skylight into the Sardine Box, but dimly, so that even by day lamps are used in the Sardine Box if you want to read.

The scene is bleak and untidy. The producer must get his effects by lighting and huge ominous shadows.

When the Curtain rises, HERON, FREWER, *and* PHILIP *are in the Sardine Box.* PHILIP *is reading, propped against the wall Left.* HERON, *on a packing-case Centre, has been reading but now lays down his book.* FREWER *is cross-legged on the floor beside* HERON, *gouging a piece of wood with a pen-knife and using the light of* HERON'S *lamp for the purpose. He is very young, a rather pathetic boy, cheerful by act of will, but by no means a warrior by nature.* HERON *is tall and dark, an efficient officer of great potential energy, but a man of profound dignity and spiritual composure.*

HERON

(*Looking at his watch*)

Still ten minutes to midnight.

PHILIP

She couldn't be back yet — not if her rendezvous
with him is where she found us.

HERON

Still we may as well get his bed made. Your job,
Dick.

FREWER

I know. I will in a second. Let me just get this
bit done.

HERON

What are you doing?

FREWER

Making something. . . . You forget that I was going
to be Michael Angelo in private life.

HERON

What in fact is it? (*Taking the piece of wood.*)

FREWER

I'll show you later. (*Gets up reluctantly.*) Now I'll
do the bed. Where do you want him to lie?

HERON

Next to me — anyhow at first. Make him a fling-
hole too.

FREWER

I can't see anything out there with only one screened
lamp. Can't I have another?

HERON

No you cannot.

58

FREWER

Can I move the one there is ? A fixed beam at floor-level is no good to me.

HERON

It's all you can have.

FREWER

But the skylight black-out is perfectly efficient.

HERON

That may be. It's not the skylight I'm afraid of. It's wall-chinks. Marie says that only this Sardine Box is dead secure with a moving light.

FREWER

I believe the outside is secure too.

HERON

Probably it is. But Marie thinks not. Anyhow it's an order.

FREWER

All right. The bed I can do. Anyone can put down straw. Making a fling-hole for him will be ticklish if I can't see.

HERON

You have the floor-beam. After eight days in this place, surely you can feel your way. If you can't, I'll come.

FREWER

Oh I can *do* it. (FREWER *goes out.*)

59

PHILIP

Dick Frewer's a helpless child.

HERON

Not so helpless.... He just doesn't like being alone.

PHILIP

He has made up his mind, poor devil, that when he gets back to England, he'll be shot down again. Of course, it's all nonsense. Still——

HERON

No, it isn't nonsense. Men often know when their number's up. Dick has to get used to it.

PHILIP

You have a pretty hard streak in you, Heron.

HERON

Have I? Ride him like a nervous colt. (*They pick up their books again.*) You'll see. When Dick comes back he'll be feeling better. (PHILIP *cannot read either and he says:*)

PHILIP

Who do you suppose this new chap is that Marie's bringing in?

HERON

She didn't tell me, and I didn't ask.

PHILIP

If he's Air Force, Dick Frewer or I may know him.

HERON

More likely a British agent being got out. That's why, as she didn't tell me, I didn't ask. Besides, this evening, she properly put me in my place. I went to hold the trap-door for her. I felt sorry for her, going out alone on this job while we sat snug in our Sardine Box ; and, like a fool, I offered to go with her.

PHILIP

But that would have been against every kind of rule.

HERON

I know. It wasn't very intelligent of me. She's probably safer alone. But she looked so grey. She seemed to have shrunk like a young tired cat. So I said : 'I'll come with you', and though she said 'No', it wasn't a very firm 'No', and I moved to follow her. Then, my God, she didn't argue. She gave an order. She said : 'Go back to the others and wait'. I *came* back.

PHILIP

She'd have given her head to have you go with her.

HERON

You like romance, don't you, Philip? I know it's your idea she's half in love with me.

PHILIP

More than half.

HERON

She's never given a sign.

PHILIP

She can't.   She's on duty.

HERON

That doesn't stop most people.

PHILIP

It stops her.

HERON

She certainly knows how to give an order — even to herself.   (HERON *rises*.)

PHILIP

Where are you off to?

HERON

I was thinking of her father down there.   (*He points to the floor.*)   It's bad enough when she's away in the daytime, doing her school job.   He always thinks she won't come back.   Now the old man must be going through hell.   I thought I'd go down to him.   Keep him company.   Divert his mind.

PHILIP

I shouldn't, Heron, if I were you.

HERON

Why not?   Old Chassaigne interests me.

PHILIP

You interest him too much.   He watches you like a terrier at a rat-hole.

62

HERON

Nonsense, Philip. He shows his teeth now and then. That's only a scholar's jealousy — very scholarly and very French. After all, he was a professor of German, and he's a poet in his own right. When it comes to German poetry, he has the whole scholarly bag of tricks down to the last footnote to a footnote — but I *hear* it as he doesn't. That puts his bristles up.

PHILIP

That isn't all. Chassaigne is obsessed. He hates Germans with a ferocity that I didn't believe could exist. (*Enter* FREWER.) Does he talk to you of Weitbrecht?

HERON

He has. I'm not blind, Philip. I know the old man's dangerous on that subject. But he can be got away from it. It's rather like making a terrier drop his rat. But he drops it.

FREWER

I asked Marie about Weitbrecht.

PHILIP

Did you indeed! It's not a popular subject in the Chassaigne family.

FREWER

So I gathered. That's what puzzled me. Weitbrecht has been dead for ages — before I was born. But he ticks on like a clock in the old boy's mind. . . . Marie said they were students together in Germany forty years ago. They worshipped each other. David and Jonathan,

Marie said. And Weitbrecht betrayed him. That's all
I know, except that — once Chassaigne himself talked
to me about him. I was talking about you, Heron. It
was queer. Chassaigne switched over quite suddenly.
At first I thought he was still talking about you. But
he said : 'He was killed in France. He is buried in
France', and he went on raving about the shame and
the dishonour of it.

HERON

But where do I come in ? I wasn't his Jonathan. I
didn't betray him or run off with his girl — which I
gather Weitbrecht did. I didn't invade France.

PHILIP

Weitbrecht is Chassaigne's devil. For him all
Germany *is* Weitbrecht. Somehow you link up. You
know Germany backwards. You know Goethe : it was
Weitbrecht's subject. You speak German . . . as a
German.

FREWER

It is true, Heron.

HERON

Philip says he's dangerous.

FREWER

I don't know about that. He's near dotty, if you
ask me. But somehow you do link up. Half the time I
didn't know whether he was talking about you or
Weitbrecht. I doubt whether he did. His terror is that
he may have a German in his house without knowing it.
To-day he's in a frazzle because this new chap's coming

— as though Weitbrecht might crawl out of his grave.
. . . But it's you he watches.

HERON

I don't blame him. Wouldn't you watch in his
place? . . . Is that bed made?

FREWER

Straw thrown down casual-like. Goering himself
wouldn't know it was a bed.

HERON

Least of all if he slept on it.

FREWER
(*To* PHILIP)

I wish you'd have a look. Just to confirm.

PHILIP

I will if you like. (*He moves towards door.*)

FREWER

And the fling-hole. Near the dresser among the pile
of empty bottles. It's full of various gubbins. Plumb
in the open. No Hun would ever rummage in it. But
have a look. I may have been too clever.

PHILIP

I'll make sure. (*Exit* PHILIP.)

HERON
(*To* FREWER, *who is obviously agitated*)

Take it quietly, Dick.

FREWER

Why do you say that?

HERON

Your piece about old Chassaigne.

FREWER

It's quite true.

HERON

I don't doubt it, but it's not important. There's no need to be worked up about it.

FREWER

I am worked up.

HERON

Why?

FREWER

You know quite well. . . . This new chap coming. Marie may bring him in at any moment now. If he's what we have been waiting for, this may be our last night here.

HERON

I don't want to go either.

FREWER

Don't you? You only say that to be kind. It doesn't rattle you. Nothing does. That's why . . . being with you has meant such a hell of a lot to me. . . . I suppose, when I get back to England, the good and great may say I'm shell-shocked or that I've lost my nerve for flying. All nonsense of course. I'm just the

66

same. It isn't even that I'm afraid of being killed. But I want to stay put long enough to grow roots.

HERON

That's what the world wants, Dick, a creative pause. When you were a child, did you have a home — I mean, a fixed, solid home?

FREWER

For a bit I did. Not long . . . I suppose what I really want is just that. How did *you* know? No more time-tables, no more journeys. To stay put night after night with no scheduled move next morning is pretty near my notion of heaven. This place has been that. . . . It's damned silly, I suppose, to be frightened of moving. My nightmare is being lost in a railway station. It's only the feeling you have in — in a warm room with people you know — of not wanting to go out into the cold.

HERON
(*After a pause*)

Death isn't like that. Dying may be.

FREWER

I wasn't talking about that.

HERON

I thought you were.

FREWER
(*Facing it*)

Yes, I was. . . . But I'm not really afraid of that any more. But I didn't want to go from here because

67

it's here I'm not afraid. I'm not as long as I can hold
on to what you said. But I shall forget that.

HERON

What *I* said?

FREWER

Two days ago. In the afternoon when it was raining,
do you remember? About the thing being 'familiar'?
Death, I mean.

HERON

I always used to have the idea myself that it must be
one of two things — either, as you said, a going out into
solitude and cold and darkness or, if it wasn't that, then
at best something unknown. I don't any longer see it
in that way but as a recall.

FREWER

From what?   To what?

HERON

From this world with its few friends and its millions
of strangers to a light and sanity which are not solitary
or cold or unknown but were familiar enough in childhood and, sometimes, are, even now. In childhood it
was a pretty steady light, though it grew more and more
distant. Even now, there are flashes of it when a tree
or a sky or even a man or a woman becomes, as you
look at them, in some way timeless, just as they were
in childhood, and reality — a kind of interior grace —
shines through appearances. I think what is coming is
a recall to that.

68

FREWER

But there's no proof.

HERON

No external proof.

FREWER

I wonder whether that was right — what you said about the things children feel. I don't remember much except — well, one thing I do remember. I used to sit up in bed shouting *Kubla Khan*. My mother was alive then. I was a frightfully ordinary little boy. It wasn't the meaning — pleasure-domes and caves of ice and all that. And it wasn't really the sound — I made a hideous din. It was a kind of . . . oh I don't know . . . a magic of some sort which let me go back into a world where I belonged and where there was nothing I was afraid of or didn't understand. Do you mean that death will be like that?

HERON

Don't say it so hopefully, Dick, as if my meaning it made it true.

FREWER

It almost does for me.

HERON

Only if you re-imagine it for yourself. (*Enter* PHILIP *as the trap-door begins to open.*)

PHILIP

They have come, I think.

FREWER

Shall I go and help with the trap-door?

HERON

Stay where you are. (*The trap-door opens. A beam of light shines up vertically.*)

MARIE

(*Emerging*)

Father, move back the lamp. It's too strong. (*The vertical light dims.* MARIE *comes up and stands, holding the trap-door.* JULIAN *follows.*) Stand still while I get the trap down.

JULIAN

Let me——

MARIE

Stand still. (*She lets down the trap. Darkness then.*) Follow me. This place is a store-room. I used it as a playroom once. Full of obstacles. Come. Take my hand. (*She leads him round and enters the Sardine Box. The three there rise.* JULIAN *is wearing pince-nez and a beret. He looks like a seedy and pedantic French official. He carries a walking-stick which has a straight handle and is attached to his wrist by a leather loop: it is a dagger-stick. Meanwhile the trap-door has opened again.* PIERRE CHASSAIGNE *comes up, and during the ensuing dialogue makes his way to the door. But time passes before his entrance. He may have been listening.*) This is Dick Frewer. This is Philip Sturgess; he's American. Both out of the air. This is Major Lang, out of Germany. We call him Heron.

JULIAN

My name is Julian Wyburton. I'll get out of fancy dress. (*He takes off his disguise.*)

FREWER
(*Ingenuously*)

Where from?

JULIAN
(*Snubbing him*)

Since you ask, last night I spent in France.

FREWER

Which Service?

JULIAN

The senior one.

FREWER

What on earth is the Navy doing in France?

JULIAN

Keeping its mouth shut. What rank are you?

FREWER

Flight-Lieutenant.

JULIAN
(*Disregarding him*)

Who is in command here?

MARIE

I am.

JULIAN

I beg your pardon. I meant under you.

MARIE

Heron is. As a naval Commander, you are senior to him. After to-night I will act through you. (CHASSAIGNE *comes in.*)

JULIAN

No, mademoiselle. He knows this outfit. I'll take my orders from him. (*To* HERON) If you agree?

HERON

As you wish, sir.

MARIE

Thank you.

JULIAN
(*To* HERON)

What is your name again? Lang?

HERON

My name is Lang. They all call me Heron.

JULIAN

Why?

HERON
(*Smiling*)

They say I look like one. I suppose I carry myself that way.

MARIE
(*With evident tenderness*)

He holds his head back. I think it's more like a knight in chess. (*Then she returns abruptly to business.*) Father, what are you doing here?

72

CHASSAIGNE

I thought I would like to meet my new guest.

MARIE

You met him as we passed through your room.

CHASSAIGNE

I like to *know* my guests. My acquaintance with
Monsieur Heron has been most instructive. (*He puts
his hand on* JULIAN'S *shoulder*.) You know, my friend,
his German is flawless. It has even the little faults that
educated Germans permit themselves. And I, as a professor, am interested in all things German.

MARIE

Father, you are leaving the room empty.

CHASSAIGNE

(*With no sign of going yet*)

That is true. I will return at once to my kennel.
. . . (*To* JULIAN) But it is interesting, is it not? You,
for example, on your journeys, play the part of a Frenchman, and these two young gentlemen also within the
limits which Nature has imposed upon them, but
Monsieur Heron, *tout naturellement*, is a German mer-
chant trading for cognac in the Charente and for oak
in the Limousin. He would even, I am told, make
little jokes with enemy pickets. He would, as you say,
pull the German leg. To do that needs great confidence.

73

JULIAN

I have found myself that to chatter is often the best way to avoid curiosity.

CHASSAIGNE

True. . . . True. . . . Admirable. . . . And, in any case, the English have always the idea to play a comedy part upon a tragic stage. It is altogether characteristic.

MARIE

Father——

CHASSAIGNE

Yes, Marie, I will go. You will say good-night to me as you descend. I shall be awake. I am always awake. (*With little jerky bows he goes out and down through the trap-door.*)

MARIE

(*To* JULIAN)

I won't keep you long to-night. You will need food and drink. I will bring it. We have special rules about food and drink. It has to be possible, in case there should be an alarm while you are eating, to remove all traces of a meal in a few seconds. A meal consists of one bowl, one spoon, one jug. You eat . . . as certain idealists would say . . . communally. The others will tell you how these . . . implements . . . are disposed of. You will find in the morning that the rest of the granary is extremely large. It is full of——

FREWER

Junk.

74

MARIE

Junk, I always forget that word — and completely disordered. There is a zinc tub there. It is half full of broken crockery, empty tins, thick water. The addition of one bowl, one spoon, one jug would not be observed by Germans. You understand me?

JULIAN

The principle — perfectly.

MARIE

You are as safe here as anywhere in France. My old father sleeps and works below. There is no access except through his room. The passages of the house are long and tortuous. He will not be taken by surprise.

JULIAN

Does he never go out?

MARIE

Seldom. . . . Never in my absence. There is a closet adjoining his room. You go down to empty slops.

JULIAN

Not otherwise?

MARIE

By rule not. There may be exceptions. The point is this — and this you must understand: my father receives Germans in his room.

JULIAN

I understand perfectly.

75

MARIE

You are quick.

JULIAN

I play your game, mademoiselle.

MARIE

As a result, the enemy regard this house as a house of collaborators. At least I hope they still do.

HERON

Why do you doubt it?

MARIE

They are a strange race. At first, if you pretend to like them, they believe it; but slowly it dawns upon them that it is unbelievable. It is some time since any Germans came to this house. That troubles me a little. Still they may come. . . . This stove-pipe runs up from my father's stove. If he knocks on it with his pipe, that is the first alarm. You keep silence; you gather what is within reach but don't move; the object at the first alarm is to risk no sound; you keep dead still and wait until my father comes up himself and gives you the all-clear. It may be quite harmless. A French visitor, perhaps. Even if it's a German, that may be harmless too. But if he shows signs of going up through the trap-door, you will get the second alarm. In that case you risk sound. It's not a great risk. My father's room lies there (*pointing Left*) beyond the stove, not directly under us. You do what Heron calls Operation Get-Away. You should be out of the granary in — how long?

HERON

We have got it down to eighty seconds up to the granary door. (*To* JULIAN) This door. We have never opened it. (*Holding lamp*) It's part of a huge granary door. The little one is all we need. It opens on to — go on, Marie. I've never been out.

MARIE

On to an outside platform with a ladder running down the wall into a courtyard. If the house is close surrounded and it's daylight, there's not much hope. Still there's a chance. Heron has instructions where to go. If the enemy searches this place and finds no sign that it was ever inhabited, it may not be impossible to pick you up again outside.

JULIAN

Operation Get-Away must have needed working out.

FREWER

For the last week we have done damned little else.

JULIAN

Still — eighty seconds! . . . Heron can drill me to-morrow. . . . (*Looking round him*) What's our living routine? Do we shave? I gather we do.

PHILIP

We don't keep shaving tackle up here. A razor comes up with breakfast. One bowl, one jug, one spoon, one razor. Goes down with breakfast.

77

JULIAN

One knife and fork?

HERON

Teeth and fingers as requisite.

MARIE

There's one other thing, Commander.

JULIAN

Yes.

MARIE

These others came through River Line headquarters in Brussels. You have come . . . by a side-track. They were warned. The discipline of the River Line deprives you of all initiative. I am in charge.

JULIAN

Certainly you are.

MARIE

But in a special way. We have through our hands men without your experience. They can speak no language but their own; they are . . . dangerously ignorant, sometimes rash. One false step by them may endanger a hundred lives — all back along the line. We found our rule on their stupidity.

JULIAN

Most rules are founded on the incompetence of the human race. . . . And the rule is?

78

MARIE

Whoever comes through the Line obeys — without reasoning, at once — whatever order is given him. If we are in a railway-carriage and I say 'sleep', you nod and snore. If we are in a street and I say 'fall in the mud', you fall instantly. It may be necessary for reasons which I alone know ; I may recognize a face which you do not. My discretion is unlimited ; your obedience absolute and instantaneous.   Do you take that ?

JULIAN

I take it.

MARIE

I want your oath.

JULIAN

I swear it.

MARIE

Thank you. . . . There is this point too. These officers carry forged identity papers. You also, no doubt. I will go through yours to-morrow. Apart from those papers which you have brought in, you carry out nothing written. Everything, even a bridge score, is burned as soon as made.

JULIAN

And how disposed of ?

MARIE

Burn it in a saucer, break up the ashes, dispose of them in what Dick calls a 'fling-hole'. Dick will show you. . . . Have you weapons ?

JULIAN

No pistol. I have this. (*He draws the blade from his walking-stick.*)

MARIE

That is quieter. . . . Now I will go and bring you food. . . . What is it, Dick?

FREWER

You're tired. I don't want to delay you. Can I ask one question?

MARIE

What is it?

FREWER

The night we came, I asked — d'you remember? — I was all in myself — I asked whether we were to move on at once or whether we could come out of top-gear. You said we were waiting for something; you didn't say what. Is this — I mean the Commander — is he the something? Do we move now?

MARIE

Not yet. (*To* JULIAN) Does that distress you?

JULIAN

Me? I can do with a few days in harbour.

FREWER

This is harbour all right.

JULIAN

What is your name?

FREWER

Frewer, sir.   Dick Frewer.

JULIAN

Sorry I snapped at you. . . . (*To* MARIE) I beg your pardon, mademoiselle.   I interrupted you.   I'm in no hurry, God knows.   In fact, when do we move?

MARIE

Transport on the last stage, straight through to the Spanish frontier, has been thrown out by this delay.   It has to be tied up ; it will take time.   There are others who will have to move into your places the night after you go and others behind them.   When the machine turns over again, it must turn over simultaneously all along the line to release the hold-up.   It isn't easy to arrange, our communications being what they are.   Once it is arranged, no revision is possible.   There's no margin for a hitch.   I hate that ; I fear it.

HERON

You mean that, when zero hour is fixed, we must go at all costs?

MARIE

I'm afraid so.

JULIAN

However unfavourable the local conditions are?   A clear night?   A full moon?

MARIE

We can calculate the moon.   Not the enemy.   Normally one can use discretion within certain limits.   This time I shall have no choice; the time-table will be inflexible. Inflexible.

PHILIP

When will it be?

MARIE

I don't know. A fortnight perhaps.

FREWER

Then we *can* come out of top-gear again.

MARIE

Poor Dick. Yes. I'll get your food, Commander.

JULIAN

Thank you, mademoiselle.

MARIE

As a matter of routine, we use Christian names. Mine is Marie.

JULIAN

Good. Then I am not 'Commander'. (*She goes out and is to be seen descending through the trap-door.*)

FREWER

She never relaxes. When we go, others come. We at least move together. She is always alone. . . . The job of a secret agent must be blazing hell.

JULIAN

Rather colder than that. . . . Heron, what are my orders for the night? Where do I fit into 'Get-Away'?

HERON

To-night you don't. To-morrow you will. To-night sleep fully dressed as you were when you arrived. Everything — but everything — in your pockets. If there's a second signal, walk out after me and follow me. . . . You can't smoke. The stubs are too obvious. (JULIAN *puts away the packet of cigarettes in his hands.*)

JULIAN

As you say. (*Picks up* FREWER'S *piece of wood. To* PHILIP) What's this?

FREWER

It's mine, sir. Pretty ingenious, I think. It's a chairleg. I've scooped it out. It fits on to this broken one. Like this. (*Fits it.*) The point is, it isn't a permanent mend. But it works. (*Sits in the chair.*) Then if the German shows up, off it comes. (*He pulls it off and flings it over the partition wall. The broken chair lolls over on its side.*) That chair hasn't been sat on for twenty years — has it? (*They all laugh.*)

JULIAN

Presumably not. And if they find the chair-leg?

FREWER

Did you know it was a chair-leg?

JULIAN

No.

FREWER

Then they won't. . . . Shall I show you your quarters?

JULIAN

Yes. Out here? . . . Don't throw that chair-leg. Place it. Why risk a clatter? (FREWER *and* JULIAN *go out.*)

PHILIP

Well?

HERON

Well, what?

PHILIP

The new boy?

HERON

He knows his job. Well, I'm going to turn in. Whose middle-watch? Yours or Dick's? I know it's not mine.

PHILIP

It's mine.

HERON

Then you can give the senior Service its supper and tuck it up in bed. (JULIAN *comes back.*)

HERON

Shut the door.

JULIAN

(*After shutting it*)

Why?

HERON

Marie doesn't trust the outside black-out at that level.

JULIAN

(*Turning up the rug and finding some cards*)

I see you play cards. Bridge or poker?

PHILIP

Both. (FREWER *comes in.*)

JULIAN

How do you dispose of them — the cards?

HERON

The rule is : We roll the rug back and play sitting on the floor. If there's an alarm, one man's cards go into his pocket and out with him. Dick Frewer has some in his pocket now. The rest throw in and the rug comes down. The enemy finds the incomplete remnants of a pack ten years old. No evidence of a recent game.

FREWER

Recent? Recent? You could plant potatoes on those bloody cards. (*During this speech,* JULIAN *has been prowling. He has come to the granary door and his hand is on the wooden latch.* PHILIP *springs towards him in alarm.*)

PHILIP

For God's sake, don't open that! The light would shine out across the courtyard into the road.

JULIAN

I don't propose to open it. When you have exercised Operation Get-Away have you ever actually raised that latch?

PHILIP

No.

JULIAN

Then I will. Wood swells.

HERON

Does it move freely?

JULIAN

It does.   (*He sits on the floor.*)

HERON

Thank you.   I had neglected that.

FREWER

(*To* JULIAN)

What made *you* think of it?

JULIAN

Naval intelligence.   We sailors are always thinking of our own skins. . . . My God, I want to smoke like a fool.

FREWER

I think that's your food coming.   (*As light begins to show through the trap-door, the stage is blacked out.*)

ACT II

SCENE 2

The same. Twelve days later. Nearly 9.30 P.M. Still daylight. FREWER *and* HERON *discovered.* HERON *writing.* FREWER *reading.*

FREWER

(*Laying down his book*)

Heron.

HERON

Yes.

FREWER

I'm sorry.   What are you writing?

HERON

(*With a smile*)

A poem.

FREWER

Then I'll shut up. . . . (*A hopeful afterthought.*) Is it important?

HERON

Anyhow it's done.

FREWER

I was going to say : Can I talk a bit?

HERON

As much as you like.

FREWER

I can't read any more. I've learnt a lot of French since I came here. Just by reading. Pretty good in the time. Twelve days since Julian came; eight before that; less than three weeks. Now, as we move to-night, I shan't ever finish this book. So I can't read it.

HERON

Yes you can. Montaigne will wait and meet you in England.

FREWER

I thought I'd got over it, Heron, but I felt sick just the same when Marie told us our transport was fixed for to-night.

HERON

Where is she now?

FREWER

Out there with Philip and Julian. At least I think so. I didn't hear her go down. (*Looks at watch.*) It's time to black-out, you know. (*He starts for the door and opens it, but* HERON *checks him.*)

HERON

Not yet. Let's have what daylight we can. . . . (FREWER *closes the door.*) Is she there still?

FREWER

Yes.

HERON

She's pretty . . . taut . . . poor Marie.

FREWER

To-day she is because it's the last day. Anyhow she was while she was telling us. But afterwards she was peaceful again. She's much less — oh I don't know — less tight-strung? — than she was when we came. She's peaceful inside herself. Although she loves you . . . or because. So am I if it comes to that. Not of course, I mean, that I'm in the same boat with you or her. She's an intellectual and I'm not.

HERON

That makes no odds once you're out of the shallows. Which am I? An intellectual or not? Don't overvalue me, Dick, I'm not in the least a leader of men.

FREWER

You are an efficient officer. I'm not even that.

HERON

Has that anything to do with it?

FREWER

I think it has. It's all part of the same thing. For most of us life is a kind of banking-account. We are always totting it up and seeing how little time there is left. And then we panic and fuss. You don't. I was learning not to, but you—— (MARIE *comes in.*)

HERON

Dick, you are identifying me with this place. Don't do that. This place is quiet and included. I am quiet and included. That is all. (*Seeing her*) Marie.

MARIE

Go on. Let me sit here and listen. It's not half-past nine yet. Nearly three hours to go. Philip says he still has scraps of paper to burn.

HERON

(*Holding up the paper on which he was writing*)
I have this.

MARIE

Time enough. . . . It's an odd feeling to sit here peacefully talking. To-morrow there will be no one; after that, new faces. For to-night everything has arranged itself smoothly. I've seldom had such long warning. All we have to do is walk out, when the time comes and——

FREWER

Is it the old rendezvous? The same ditch where you first picked us up?

MARIE

Yes, thank heaven. I believe you have almost an affection for that ditch.

FREWER

I have. Like the beginning of the holidays. When the war's over, on a sunshiny day after a very good lunch, I shall stop my enormous Rolls-Royce beside that ditch, and I shall say — But I don't suppose I shall. Everyone says 'after the war'. What the hell will happen?

MARIE

Not too much, I hope. Quite enough has happened in the last few years.

HERON

I believe Marie has been converted to my idea of a creative pause.

MARIE

I didn't need converting. I teach history. After Napoleon there wasn't another world war for a hundred years : which, after all, is something. Talleyrand and Metternich weren't fools.

HERON

No, Marie, indeed they weren't, but their problem was only a part of ours. (JULIAN *comes in to fetch something, and, still standing, pauses to listen.*) The modern world is far more exhausted than theirs. Our trouble isn't so much that men choose wrong policies as that they are losing the power to choose at all ; like a man who is driving a car hell for leather — and has been for half a century — and whose steering-gear has gone wrong. Doesn't even the most progressive driver pause then ?

FREWER

It's the same with trees.

MARIE

Trees ?

FREWER

Fruit-trees. My father grew them. He said : 'Don't *bother* trees or women ; if you do, the sap don't rise.'

JULIAN

That's the odd thing about this place. The sap does rise. When I came, I was hellish impatient. I pestered you — didn't I, Marie? — about plans for getting on. But once I grasped that there was nothing on earth I could do about it, I found — I mean as regards my own job — that I could for once think back to the roots of policy instead of bothering my head about to-morrow's ways and means.

MARIE

Your job!

JULIAN

Why not?

MARIE

You are incorrigible, aren't you, Julian? You think of everything — even of the sap rising — in terms of your own Service . . . just as you everlastingly carry your dagger-stick in your hand. Why do you? You aren't going to be attacked here.

JULIAN

Habit.

MARIE

But you might put it down sometimes.

JULIAN

Why do women lose their hand-bags?

FREWER

But you needn't sleep with it!

JULIAN

Needn't I? Why do husbands lose their wives? (*He goes out.*)

HERON

(*With a laugh. To* MARIE)

How you bait him about his Service! You are just as concentrated on yours.

MARIE

Perhaps that's why. I wanted to forget for half an hour. Everything that can be done has been done. Everything is set for to-night. I wanted to think of something else. Or not think.

FREWER

(*To* MARIE)

Like Heron. . . . D'you know what he was doing just now?

MARIE

(*To* HERON)

What were you doing?

FREWER

Writing a poem.

HERON

(*Making a spill of his poem*)

Making spills.

FREWER

But Heron, do you really write poetry? Do you publish it, I mean? Ought I to have heard of you and all that?

HERON

Heard of me? Certainly not.

FREWER

What on earth do you write poetry about? Spring and love and so on?

HERON

About nothing on earth — at least I suppose not. Are you by any chance a musician?

FREWER

I like it. Why?

HERON

Music is *about* something, but not in the same way that what is written in words is about something, and there are people who don't need to have even the physical sound on the drums of their ears. They read a score silently and compose silently. And often the music composed silently is about nothing that is visible or touchable or audible : it's about something, inside nature and beyond the senses, which isn't even thinkable except in music — and imperfectly, I suppose, even in music. Why shouldn't poetry move towards that — away from the logic that ties words to appearances?

FREWER

Kubla Khan did that.

MARIE

Did it? I have never understood *Kubla Khan*.

FREWER

But it's dead clear! It's as clear as a nursery rhyme.

MARIE

(*To* HERON)

Is it? I am French, of course.

FREWER

I think I see now. (*To* HERON) About something, you mean, so far *inside* that you have to stop thinking before you can let it come through.

HERON

'If I but had the eyes and ears
To read within what now appears,
Then should I see in every face
An innocent, interior grace,
And, as the clouds of thought unfurled,
Be native of the golden world.'

FREWER

You must see that, Marie, you must!

MARIE

Must I? At least I'm intellectual enough to know that I'm half-blind.

HERON

Dear Marie.

MARIE

What did you say?

HERON

Dear Marie. (*He takes her hand and almost at once releases it. It means much to her that he should have spoken those words, and, for a moment, she covers her face.*

FREWER, *who has twisted round and has not been looking at them, goes on :)*

FREWER

I think I do see now. I suppose I shan't to-morrow morning. . . . And even now, I don't really see. (*He turns back to* HERON.) Poetry *must* be about something. It can't just be about the music you don't hear and the things you don't touch and——

HERON

And the food you don't eat?

FREWER

Well, yes, but why do you say that?

HERON

'For he on honey-dew hath fed
And drunk the milk of Paradise.'

Why not? Sound without hearing, truth without arguing, love without loving, loss without losing. Why not? Isn't that a subject for poetry? You can call it nonsense rhymes if you like. (HERON *strikes a light and is about to burn the spill he has made.*)

MARIE

But that — in your hand — have you just written it?

HERON

Not long ago.

MARIE

Is it — the verses you just said?

HERON

No, indeed.

MARIE

Do you know it by heart — your own poem, I mean?

HERON

No.

MARIE

But you are starting to-night.   All papers have to be burned.

HERON

That's what I was doing.

FREWER

I do see what Marie means.   What's the good of writing it?

HERON

To write it.

FREWER

If it was ever going to be published — or not even published; if *anyone* was going to read it, even yourself afterwards — but as things are . . .

HERON

Better as things are. . . . Not better; the same. (*He lights the spill.*) I haven't the least desire to keep it or anything.   It makes no difference what you keep. The thing was there before you had it, and is still there when it seems to have gone.   (*The trap-door opens.*)

MARIE

Listen. What is that? (PHILIP, *from the dark interior, appears at the trap-door as* CHASSAIGNE *emerges.*)

CHASSAIGNE

Which of them are you?

PHILIP

Sturgess. The American.

CHASSAIGNE

Marie is here?

PHILIP

You know she is.

CHASSAIGNE

I want her urgently — urgently.

PHILIP

Come then. She is in here. (*They enter through the door of the Sardine Box.* JULIAN *follows. The meditative atmosphere has suddenly changed.*)

MARIE

What is it, father?

CHASSAIGNE

The enemy is moving. Everything is changed. This message came. Read it. (*Hands paper to* MARIE.)

MARIE

It is in cipher.

THE RIVER LINE

CHASSAIGNE

I am not a fool. I have deciphered it. On the back it is *en clair*. Read it! Read it! (MARIE *turns the paper and reads silently*.)

MARIE

If they are moving, your room must not be empty. Go back, father.

CHASSAIGNE

In face of that you will not start?

MARIE

I will decide.

CHASSAIGNE

You cannot go. Virac is too far.

MARIE

Go back, father.

CHASSAIGNE

Ah well, I go. (CHASSAIGNE *goes*. MARIE *waits until the trap-door is closing*.)

MARIE

I'm sorry. This is difficult. Plans have changed. This is a message from farther up the Line. The road which passes our ditch outside Blaise has become unsafe. You can't be picked up there.

JULIAN

In what way unsafe?

MARIE

The enemy will be moving over it to-night. Your transport has been diverted through Virac St. Just. We

99

are to be at Rendezvous 46 — it is a grocer's shop in Virac — not earlier than one-five, not later than one-fifteen, in the morning. The car will have two others on board, by-passing Blaise. At one-fifteen it goes forward.

JULIAN

(*Looking at watch*)

It is now — nine-thirty-seven. Three hours and three-quarters. How far is Virac?

MARIE

Forty-three kilometres.

JULIAN

Twenty . . . seven miles?

MARIE

You still think in miles. . . .

PHILIP

In English, French, or American, it is impossible on foot.

MARIE

That is the point. Secondary transport from Blaise to Virac has to be found.

FREWER

If a car could be stolen——

MARIE

It must not be stolen.

FREWER

Borrowed then. You could take us to Virac and drive the car back.

MARIE

I cannot drive. In any case, I must not leave Blaise.

FREWER

We could drive, and scrap it short of Virac.

MARIE

No, Dick. A car stolen from Blaise and scrapped at at Virac. That would stir up the hornets' nest. No.

FREWER

Then the thing's not possible. . . . I say, Heron, it really is time to do our black-out now.

HERON

Yes. Do it. (FREWER *goes out to obey, and a little later the blind comes down over the skylight and the stage darkens. While* FREWER *is going,* HERON *at once takes up the thread, saying to* MARIE:) Is there secondary transport?

MARIE

At present none. I have to find it. There are two possibilities — Dessaix and Félix, both loyal men.

HERON

Part of the River Line?

MARIE

No. But part of the Resistance. They know me. They will help if they can. Dessaix is a foreman at the brick-works; he can put his hand on a truck. Or there is a small Citroën belonging to the municipality. Monsieur Félix is an official; he has the garage key. Either might go. To them the risks are enormous. Notice is so short, they have no chance to prepare cover. Either might take the risk. It depends on how they are placed to-night. It may be impossible for either of them.

JULIAN

You mean you are going to ask them?

MARIE

I must. I must.

JULIAN

The risk to you is enormous. Suppose they rat.

MARIE

They will not, I think. . . . I must have transport for you.

JULIAN

Listen. What would happen if we didn't start?

MARIE

If you stayed here, the whole Line would pile up. Within twenty-four hours I should have eight men on my hands. The block at this end would be disastrous.

HERON

Look, Marie. Neither Julian nor I knows the detail of the network. Both of us are talking without our book. We are under your orders and we take your orders. Still, consider this. The danger to the Line of an improvised start may be greater than the danger of a pile-up at this end.

MARIE

You wish not to start?

HERON

I haven't the knowledge on which to decide. My intuition says No.

MARIE

(*To* JULIAN)

And you?

JULIAN

I agree.

MARIE

Why?

JULIAN

I think that, in going to Félix and Dessaix, you are running an intolerable risk. You put yourself in their hands.

MARIE

I personally?

JULIAN

Marie, I — all of us here — when we are gone and you are left behind——

MARIE

Thank you. I know. You are kind. But it isn't your job to protect me. It is my job to post my parcels.

PHILIP

The whole question is——

MARIE

There is no question. If I can get Félix or Dessaix, you will start. I shall try Dessaix first. The approach must be made with the utmost caution. To get him alone, I may have to wait and wait. If he has company, I must make a plausible excuse, leave him, watch the house, and return when his visitor has gone. Félix may be even more difficult. He has a wife. . . . It will take time.

JULIAN

There's time enough. Three and three-quarter hours?

MARIE

Work it back. Virac at latest one-fifteen. Allow a minimum of forty-five minutes on the road. Eight minutes from this house to the place where Dessaix's car will pick you up if it picks you up at all. Total fifty-three. We must leave this granary not an instant later than twelve-twenty-two.

HERON

Twelve-twenty-two.

MARIE

That leaves no margin. An average of sixty kilometres is almost impossible on the Virac road at night. I need fifteen minutes more. We may have it. Take twelve-twenty-two as an extreme dead-line.

HERON

That gives you a little over two hours and a half to be back here.

MARIE

More than enough, if things go well. If not . . .
Synchronize. (*She holds out her watch.*)

HERON

(*Comparing his*)

Nine-forty-one.

MARIE

Is it understood? You will be ready to start at sixty-
seconds notice.

HERON

Less.

MARIE

I may, if I have luck, be back in under an hour. If
not — oh well. I am sorry. It is not intelligent to
operate without a margin.

HERON

We live in a world in which we have all agreed to be
fooled by the clock.

MARIE

When I return, there may be no chance to say good-
bye. So I say good-bye . . . to you all . . . now.
(*Stage black-out.*)

ACT II

SCENE 3

Three minutes to midnight. Skylight blacked out. Floor beam showing backstage. In the Sardine Box, FREWER'S improvised chair-leg is fitted to the armchair. Behind a low packing-case Right Centre, HERON stands facing the audience. On the packing-case, six inches to Left of its right edge, is a dark-lantern, its beam shining leftward along the packing-case. To the Right of the packing-case, close to it, is miscellaneous debris, which, together with the right edge of the packing-case, is in the black shadow of the dark lantern. PHILIP is squatted at the Left end of the packing-case.

Upstage, against the wall, is another lamp, silhouetting HERON. Between this lamp and HERON, JULIAN is moving about gathering things, chiefly books.

PHILIP

(To JULIAN)

I thought you said you were through.

JULIAN

I am, all but my make-up.

PHILIP

Make-up? *(He lights paper in tin bowl. It flares up and smokes.)*

106

JULIAN

Pince-nez, beret — I have on these damned pointed boots. All dressed up and — no means of going. Marie has been away too long. I don't like it.

HERON

Two hours and more. Obviously the first man wouldn't play. It's getting late even for the second.

JULIAN

She may just not come back at all. In which case . . . (*But that sentence won't complete itself and he swerves from it violently.*) The debris in this room might be more evenly distributed. Too many books. I'll take some out. . . . (*And he swerves again.*) What are you chaps doing?

PHILIP

Emptying our pockets.

JULIAN

Looks like a sacrificial altar. . . . One thing about the River Line : it teaches you to burn your love-letters. (*Goes out.*)

PHILIP

I have very little outside the wallet I'm entitled to carry. This caricature that Dick gave me. I let that go reluctantly. But go it must. It has English balloons coming out of its mouth. (*While* PHILIP *is speaking and burning,* HERON *is searching his own pockets, making a little pile on the ledge of the packing-case behind the lamp. From the pile, he takes a sheet and hands it to* PHILIP.)

HERON

Burn them one by one. We don't want the ash to
fly. . . . (*He takes up and hands over another sheet.*)
And that. (*And now he comes to some blue sheets of note-
paper, taken from his pocket by mistake. These he rapidly
secretes. As he does so, an envelope is flicked off the
packing-case into the dark debris on his left. Neither sees
this. Nor does half the audience. But they will learn.*)
That is all. (*He hands over one more sheet.*)

PHILIP

It's odd how one clings to paper. Strictly we oughtn't
to have had even these. They ought to have been burned
'as soon as made'. . . . Are you sure that's all?

HERON

Quite sure.

PHILIP

Let's go through our pockets once more. (*They do
so, but* HERON *does not produce the sheets we have just seen
him put away.*)

PHILIP

All clear.

HERON

I have nothing.

PHILIP
(*Taking up the bowl*)

I'll dispose of these ashes. (*He carries them out, leaving the door ajar.* HERON *waits a little, thinks, hesitates,
then takes out the blue letter and kneels by the lamp.* PHILIP

has appeared in the door and starts back from what he sees.
The clock in the village begins to strike midnight.

With a pencil, HERON *swiftly adds some amendment.*
Then he claps his hands to his pockets, obviously searching
for something he cannot find. He lifts the edge of the carpet,
still searching. Then, putting away the folded leaves, rises
hastily and sees PHILIP.

PHILIP

What are you looking for?

HERON

A — a piece I wrote which I don't remember having
burned. I may have done or it may still be out here.
(*He goes out.* PHILIP *follows him with his eyes. He has*
seen too much. Suspicion is flowing in upon him. He
wavers in hesitation, then sees the envelope lying in the dark
of the lantern, darts for it, reads it. Meanwhile CHASSAIGNE
has been quietly coming up through the trap-door. He
now enters.)

CHASSAIGNE
(*Who is in a state of distressed agitation*)

When is she coming back? She gave me no time!

PHILIP
(*Wheeling, startled by the voice*)

You!

CHASSAIGNE

What is that in your hand? Are you not leaving
to-night. Do you carry papers?

PHILIP

We have been burning them.

109

CHASSAIGNE

Good. . . . When do you expect her?

PHILIP

Twelve-twenty-two.

CHASSAIGNE

It is close.

PHILIP

(*Struggling for decision*)

Go back, for God's sake! What are you doing here? (CHASSAIGNE *turns towards the door.* PHILIP *is in an agony of choice.*)

PHILIP

Wait (CHASSAIGNE *turns.*) I have no choice. None. . . . Read that.

CHASSAIGNE

(*Snatching the envelope, falling on one knee to read it*)

Frau Gustav Keller, Leipzig, Lotzestrasse 73! . . . Leipzig! Leipzig! This is not your handwriting. It is his! (*On his feet, throwing out an arm, trembling and pointing.*) It is his! Heron! Where is the letter?

PHILIP

There is no letter. . . . On him, I think. . . . He dropped the envelope. He was looking for it.

CHASSAIGNE

The envelope is enough. Leipzig!

PHILIP

Quiet. We have only an instant. All the evidence

runs together now. Heron. . . . My God! It is unbelievable.

CHASSAIGNE

My young friend, a man need not be base to be your enemy.

PHILIP

The right course is to tell him, to tell the others, to give him a chance to——

CHASSAIGNE

You cannot. This is not a court of law. The road is not thirty yards away. If he is warned, if there is a struggle, an outcry, he will call attention to this house.

PHILIP

But he can't go forward into Spain.

CHASSAIGNE

That is for Marie to decide.

PHILIP

How can I tell her? When she returns, there will be no time. If I try to tell her then——

CHASSAIGNE

I will tell her before she comes to you.

PHILIP

She will come expecting to start instantly. She may not listen to you. If there were time, I could tell her. Somehow she must find a way to keep him here while inquiries are made. Can you make her understand that?

III

CHASSAIGNE

Inquiries? She will understand, my young friend. *Il ne passera pas.* Lotzestrasse. Leipzig. Give me that envelope. It is enough. (*He tucks it away as the others enter.*)

HERON

You, monsieur. Here?

CHASSAIGNE

I came for a little company.

HERON

To-night? Your room is unguarded.

CHASSAIGNE

That is true. I am a thoughtless old man. I go at once. (*He goes out and down through the trap-door.*)

JULIAN

Are we all set? (*All except* PHILIP *have their equipment or disguise for travel. The difference is very slight — a raincoat, a hat,* JULIAN'S *pince-nez.*) These things, I believe, are the best of all disguises if you have my kind of face and you put them on wide — so that they draw up the flesh under the eyes. They narrow the whole face. Stick out your teeth, stick out your neck, stoop a bit and you are transformed into a bureaucratic rabbit.

PHILIP

I have a hat to get and a brief-case.

112

HERON

Get them. . . . Get out the cards, Dick. (PHILIP *goes.*)

FREWER

Cards? Now?

HERON

It's twelve-ten. Twelve minutes to zero. We may as well play a hand. Better than doing nothing and waiting for the kettle to boil. (FREWER *brings out cards from his pocket.* JULIAN *turns the rug back and gathers other cards from under it. Together, he and* FREWER *make up the pack.* HERON *meanwhile is wandering about, looking for his vanished envelope.*)

JULIAN

What are you looking for so diligently?

HERON

Making sure nothing's left behind. (*He sits down ready to play. He is facing the audience.* JULIAN *drops down on his right.* FREWER *is on* HERON's *left, and is seen in left-quarter-face. When* PHILIP *comes in, he sits on* JULIAN's *right in a position from which, by shifting a little when* MARIE *comes, he can make room for her between him and* JULIAN.)

JULIAN

Partners as we sit?

FREWER

I shan't be much good to you at nine minutes to zero hour.

JULIAN

She's running it fine.

FREWER

She may not have got either car. We may not start.
(PHILIP *comes in and sits down.* FREWER *goes on.*) I
remember once, just as I was starting back from leave,
I got an extension——

PHILIP

Why are we playing bridge? I can't play bridge
now. . . ..

HERON

Poker if you like.

JULIAN

We are only four.

HERON

Never mind.   Deal.

FREWER

We haven't any kind of chips.

PHILIP

Deal, for God's sake, chips or no chips.   (JULIAN
deals.)

HERON

Assume my ante.   I'm shy.

FREWER

Assume my straddle.

JULIAN

Cards?

HERON

Four to the joker.

JULIAN

Wake up, Dick. Cards?

FREWER

Two.

PHILIP

Three.

JULIAN

Dealer Three. Who bets? . . . Philip? (*The trap-door rises.* MARIE *begins to come in.*)

PHILIP

One shilling.

JULIAN

I'll see that.

HERON

I make it — oh what does it matter — five shillings. Five bob shy.

FREWER

I'm in — and shy. We're all shy. This is ghost-poker.

PHILIP

I make it ten. What? What did you say?

FREWER

It's three minutes to zero.

JULIAN

I'm away. (*Throws in his cards.*)

HERON

Fifteen.

FREWER

I'm away.

PHILIP
(*To* HERON)
We two. . . . Twenty. Your bet. (MARIE *now comes in. They stir, half-rise.*)

HERON

Now?

MARIE

No. Not now. There's been a hitch.

JULIAN

What has happened? (*Leaps to her side.*) You look half-dead. My dear, what has happened?

MARIE

Sit down. Go on with your game. (*They obey.*)

PHILIP
(*To* HERON)
Only you and I are left in, Heron. Your bet. (MARIE *sits on her heels between* PHILIP *and* JULIAN. *Nerving herself to act, she drags her hands across her face. She is shaking violently.*)

JULIAN

Marie, what have they done to you? (*He moves towards her.*)

MARIE
(*Throwing back her head*)
No. No. No. For one moment leave me alone.
(*She covers her face again.*)

HERON
Twenty-five.

PHILIP
Thirty.

HERON
Forty.

PHILIP
Fifty. (*And now* MARIE *is raised up on her knees.*)

MARIE
Commander. (JULIAN *stiffens to extreme alertness.
She looks steadily into* HERON'S *face and he at her without
flinching. She raises her arm at* HERON.) Kill that man.
(JULIAN, *with a violent indrawing of breath, draws his dagger
and kills* HERON. MARIE *watches and watches. They are
all upright —* JULIAN *last.* HERON *raises himself in a final
agony. His face is, for a moment, visible. Then he falls
back.*)

JULIAN
Why?

MARIE
Now go. Leave everything. My father will deal with
the lamp and . . . Go. (*They go out of the room,*
FREWER *last. At the door, he turns back alone, wrenches
his chair-leg off and disposes of it. Then he catches up the
others and the trap-door closes behind him. After a moment's*

pause, the trap-door opens again. CHASSAIGNE *comes up.*
The envelope is in his hand. He stoops over the body,
dragging the lamp towards it.)

CHASSAIGNE

Leipzig. (*He rifles the pockets and brings out the letter*
on blue paper.)

CHASSAIGNE

Ah! (*With great avidity, crouched by the lamp, he*
unfolds the letter.)

CHASSAIGNE
(*Rises*)

We shall see. We shall see. (*He pauses in his*
reading to stare at the body and jabs at it with his foot.)

CHASSAIGNE

One more.

Curtain

ACT III

ACT III

Scene 1

The lawn of Act I. The next morning — Saturday.
PHILIP STURGESS, *finishing breakfast in the garden, is
pouring out his last cup of coffee.* JULIAN *comes in, wearing
old country clothes.*

JULIAN

Still breakfasting.   You are a man of leisure.

PHILIP

My last cup.   I gather from the looks of it, you and
Marie finished long ago.

JULIAN

Have you seen her?

PHILIP

For a moment.

JULIAN

I have housekeeping news to report.   News for you
too.   I had to go down early into Tarryford.   On the
bridge, I met the Iron Duke.   Your young woman has
her sailing orders.

PHILIP

My God, since when?

JULIAN

An hour ago. Her passage was confirmed by telephone from London. She's packing now. America will have to intervene swiftly.

PHILIP

She can't pack! She was coming out with me this morning. She was to pick me up here (*looks at watch*) about now and we were to — When does she go?

JULIAN

Sunday.

PHILIP

To-morrow!

JULIAN

Leaves here to-morrow. One full day in London. Sails Tuesday. From your air of . . . controlled panic . . . do I gather that yesterday evening wasn't satisfactory? You followed us at so discreet a distance that I thought you were making progress?

PHILIP

I was. But not enough. I felt . . . you'll think me wrong . . . that first she must know more about me. . . . Or, if you like, that I must know more about myself.

JULIAN

Beware of a sick conscience. Never cry over spilt blood — anyhow not aloud. . . . So you told her the whole tale?

PHILIP

Do you mind?

JULIAN

N-no. Not if you are going to marry her. Are you?

PHILIP

I shall find out this morning.

JULIAN

What did you call Heron?

PHILIP

Heron. The other name, Lang, was false. It never enters my mind. Anyhow what odds would it make? (*Enter* MARIE.)

JULIAN

To her none, I grant you. But names travel. Is there anything (*he hesitates and continues with a certain reluctance because he is now, in effect, lying*) to be gained by letting the enemy know what became of their agents?

PHILIP

The enemy! The enemy! The enemy! You are obsessed, Julian. Who are the enemy?

MARIE

I will tell you. They are those who hate God, who despise the human person, who deny the liberty of thought. It is not a question of nationality. Still, dear Philip, the Rhine is not as broad as the Atlantic. Nor are the Oder and the Neisse. There are always enemies of France in the world, and of England — and of America, too. O thou of too much faith! The herd peoples are still moving westward. Twice the flood has been thrown back. There is a third to come. Be silent, be silent, be silent until Armageddon is *over*. It is by no means over yet.

JULIAN

(*Steadying her hand with his*)

Marie believes in keeping her powder dry.

MARIE

Eh bien, je suis française. (*She begins to pile the breakfast things on the tray.*)

JULIAN

Mrs. Muriven and Miss Barton are coming this evening.

MARIE

(*In consternation*)

This evening? To dinner?

JULIAN

You are indeed French.

MARIE

But there will be nothing worth eating. . . . Nevertheless, I will arrange.

JULIAN

I said you were adorably and competently French. (*Rises.*) I must get on with my job. . . . In fact, my dear, you may rest in peace. Mrs. Muriven is considerately English. She refused dinner. They will come up afterwards. The girl is leaving to-morrow. (*He goes out.*)

MARIE

Valerie is leaving to-morrow?

PHILIP

Not if I can prevent it. Passages can be cancelled. (*He helps her with the breakfast things.*)

MARIE

Ah, Philip, don't press too hard for that. If she has given her word to go to South Africa, she will wish to go, at least until her brother has had time to make other plans.

PHILIP

But an engagement to marry cancels all engagements.

MARIE

That is extremely untrue. (*She is carrying the tray towards the drawing-room.*) Besides, she is English.

PHILIP

English?

MARIE

(*With a smile, over her shoulder*)

They like to keep their word in strict order of priority. (*She carries out the tray through the drawing-room.* PHILIP *follows with spirit-lamp and coffee-pot.* VALERIE *enters up-Left, having come across the front of the house. She sits tranquilly on the stone seat.* PHILIP *returns.*)

PHILIP

Your passage has come through?

VALERIE

Commander Wyburton told you?

PHILIP

Nevertheless we go for our walk? . . . Or stay here?
. . . You are tired after last night?

VALERIE

No. I was happy last night. Why were you afraid?
You were, you know. I told you so then.

PHILIP

I answered you then. (*Wanting an excuse to laugh.*)
You always say 'you know'. I begin to think I know
very little.

VALERIE

You are a queer creature.

PHILIP

I? I'm the most ordinary creature on— After all,
who does know the whole of any story? Particularly
of a story in which they themselves have taken part.
Ought I to loathe and despise Heron?

VALERIE

Why should you?

PHILIP

He was, in effect, a spy.

VALERIE

Commander Wyburton was a spy. One cannot
despise brave men.

PHILIP

It is . . . interesting . . . to hear you say that.
Marie and Julian would say it, but they are professionals,
they are hard.

VALERIE

Hard? Have you watched their eyes — even their
hands? His way of reaching out and just not touching
her. They give me the feeling of two people with a
wall of glass between them which . . . isn't there. And
yet something is.

PHILIP

(*Quoting*)

'Silences.' Marie's word. I don't pretend to understand it. . . .

VALERIE

There's a part of the story I don't understand. Did
Heron in fact send home an earlier letter? You saw him
buy stamps. But did he send a letter?

PHILIP

In fact we know he did.

VALERIE

Did you see him?

PHILIP

No one saw him, but Frewer knew of it. Frewer told
us in our ship on the way home from Barcelona. Heron
had told him quite openly what he was doing. One of
his fellow-prisoners, an English Major, had been dying
in camp. He had a sister in Leipzig, married to a German.
Heron, when he escaped, was to carry messages in his

head, and write to Leipzig from France. No censorship that way. Frewer didn't doubt the story at the time.

VALERIE

But, Philip, if Heron had been genuine, surely his right course would have been to ask for the letter to be read and sent?

PHILIP

By the River Line agents? To give a letter to one of them was to take a hundred-to-one chance against its being sent. They wouldn't risk it. That, anyhow, is how Frewer saw it, and I don't blame him. He had no possible reason to suspect Heron. One doesn't look for one's partner to cheat at cards.

VALERIE

And the second letter? Marie must have seen and read that.

PHILIP

Her old father took it off Heron's body. It was stuck with his blood. I can't discuss it with Marie. All I know about it is through Julian. It appeared to be harmless. Outwardly, at any rate, it was written to a woman about her brother. Marie says, too, that, when she had it tested for cipher by the River Line cryptographers, the early results were negative. Beyond that she hasn't gone; maybe she can't; she herself was arrested soon afterwards.

VALERIE

And the woman? the sister in Leipzig?

PHILIP

No trace, I gather. But that goes for nothing.
Leipzig is in the Russian zone.

VALERIE

Oh, Philip, all the things that used to be wild melodrama have become commonplaces. It's a kind of
madness. You and Julian Wyburton and Heron himself all doing right and inevitable things——

PHILIP

But were they? That's the whole point.

VALERIE

They were right and inevitable on that plane of
insane violence.

PHILIP

And dead against every intuition of our personal lives.

VALERIE

That is why I said : 'madness'.

PHILIP

But the world has gone through its periods of violence
before.

VALERIE

Different from this. Far less penetrating. There
weren't the communications to carry the perpetual
thought of it. Now it comes out of every wireless-box
all day and half the night. Then there were huge areas
of life in which men thought in terms of their flocks and
herds, their families, their village——

PHILIP

Violence marched into their village now and then.

VALERIE

Only as a special misfortune.   Now violence is a
condition of thought.   That is new.

PHILIP

If so, it may produce new remedies.

VALERIE

Must there be a 'remedy'?   Everyone assumes that
there must be a Utopia round the corner.

PHILIP

Isn't there?   Not even a Christian Utopia?

VALERIE

Not even a Christian Utopia.   Not in political terms.

PHILIP

Then what does it mean to say: 'Thy Kingdom
come.   Thy will be done, *in earth*'?

VALERIE

What does it mean to say: 'The Kingdom of God is
within you'?

PHILIP

We are asking questions, not answering them.

VALERIE

I think that is all we can do. Making ourselves eyes to see in the dark ; not asserting beforehand what we shall see.

PHILIP

'Preferring——'

VALERIE

Preferring ?

PHILIP

I was trying to remember the phrase. It was on one of the scraps of paper we burned that night. 'Preferring knowledge before power, and wisdom before knowledge and love before wisdom ; but preferring also the faculty of wonder before the faculty of sight.'

VALERIE

(*Listening to an echo but not yet recognizing it as such*)

Did he write that ? (*And the actress, with a puzzled gaze from* PHILIP *to help her, leaves us to wonder who* VALERIE *meant by 'he' — her brother or Heron or, almost, both ?* PHILIP *leaves the question as needing no answer and sits beside her. Suddenly she turns to him and lays her hand on his hand with a movement so simple and spontaneous that he is astonished by it. She says :*) There is nothing to fear.

PHILIP

You put your hand on mine !

VALERIE

To tell you there is nothing to fear. (*She takes back her hand naturally.*)

131

PHILIP

Since we have been together this morning and have
been, in a way, so near, so much nearer even than we
were last night, I am not afraid of anything except . . .
of myself. Perhaps I am just one of those people who
make drastic decisions because they are themselves inde-
cisive and have a kind of false naïveté because they aren't
genuinely simple. If so, I'm not of much use to you.
Still, I might grow. I did in that granary. I have since
I knew you. . . . Suddenly one meets someone who
isn't muddy or cloudy, someone who — you said once
that your brother had . . . serenity. You loved him
for that. I'm not calm, I'm not unruffled.

VALERIE

But serene doesn't mean only 'calm'. It means also
'clear, translucent, with light shining through'.

PHILIP

Like you. Valerie, listen. . . . What have you
there?

VALERIE

(*Hands him the case she has taken from her bag*)
That is my brother's photograph. (*The photograph
is enclosed in a case fastened by a strap. He fumbles with
it, but, his thought being elsewhere, does not instantly open
it.*) No. Turn it over. It snaps open.

PHILIP

(*Taking her hand as she stretches it out towards the case*)
Sit quite still. I'm not looking at you. You know
better what I am than I know myself. You must decide

. . . peacefully . . . whether, being so different. . . .
Last night, before I told you that story, I asked you not
to take your hand away and now—— (*He drops her hand,
and draws away from her. The photograph-case has fallen
open. Silence.*)

VALERIE

Philip!

PHILIP

(*With a violent effort he stands up. He has gone
suddenly into reverse.*)
What was his name?

VALERIE

John — John Lang.

PHILIP

Not your name?

VALERIE

I told you : he was my half-brother.

PHILIP

How old was he?

VALERIE

He would have been now — thirty-three.

PHILIP

And that uniform. What regiment is it?

VALERIE

Philip, what is the matter?

PHILIP

It's extraordinary how he carries his head. Upright.
Almost backward, you'd say. Even in the photograph
you can see — Can I keep it?

VALERIE
(*Surprised*)

Yes. Why?

PHILIP

It is . . . almost of you. A memento.

VALERIE

My dear, what is wrong?

PHILIP

Nothing.

VALERIE

But there is something.

PHILIP

No.

VALERIE

You look ill? Why? What has happened?

PHILIP
(*Takes her in his arms but does not kiss her*)

Once . . . (*Releases her, moves abruptly away towards
the drawing-room. Stops. Looks back.*)

VALERIE
(*Quietly*)

Something has happened. If you can, tell me.

134

PHILIP

Is it true you leave to-morrow?

VALERIE

Yes.

PHILIP

Then this is . . . good-bye.

VALERIE

(*Accepting this without understanding it*)

Good-bye, dear Philip. . . . I mean it in the old sense.

PHILIP

The old sense? (*He does not wait for an answer but goes out.*)

VALERIE

(*Alone. She is standing near the stone seat*)

God be with you, my dearest, in all your strange troubles, and with me in mine. (*Exhausted by shock she sits down, staring before her, making herself eyes to see in the dark; and says to herself:*)

' If I but had the eyes and ears
To read within what now appears,
Then should I see in every face
An innocent, interior grace,
And, as the clouds of thought unfurled,
Be native of the golden world.'

If I but had the eyes—— (*She rises now, covers her eyes, uncovers them, lifts her head, begins to walk away.* JULIAN *enters up-Left in her path.*)

JULIAN

Alone?

VALERIE

Yes. (*In a light tone*) I must go home and pack. (*They pass.*)

JULIAN

See you to-night. (*He goes to the table. Picks up a paper.* PHILIP *re-enters.*)

JULIAN

What has happened? I met her going.

PHILIP

What did you say?

JULIAN

Nothing, I couldn't. But I saw . . . Oh, I said something to pass it off. I said : 'See you to-night'.

PHILIP

She won't come to-night. . . . Sit down, Julian. I have something to say. . . . Sit down for God's sake. (*They sit at the table.*) Will you consider that? It's an interesting photograph. She gave it to me. It's her brother. . . . No, turn it over. It snaps open. (JULIAN *opens it, stares, but gives no sign.*) Well, Julian?

JULIAN

How much does she know? . . . How much does Miss Barton know?

PHILIP

No more than she did. That her brother is gone, presumed dead.

JULIAN

But that Heron was her brother?

PHILIP

No.

JULIAN

(*Challenging what he thinks is a lie*)

Then why were you so sure she wouldn't come here to-night?

PHILIP

(*Angry*)

Why in heaven's name do you ask that? What does it matter? You look at a photograph which tells you that the man we killed was a loyal officer, and all you ask is how much Valerie knows and why she should not dine here! Isn't that a personal matter between her and me?

JULIAN

I have known for nearly four years that we were mistaken. As soon as I reached England, I sent for Lang's *dossier*. It tallied beyond question. I have seen that photograph before.

PHILIP

And you wouldn't tell me?

JULIAN

I have told no one.

PHILIP

(*Angrier*)

But when you saw what was happening between

Valerie and me, surely, if you are not inhuman, your precious rule of secrecy——

JULIAN

Listen. Get this straight. That Heron was genuine I have known for nearly four years. That he was her brother I have this moment learned. The name of Barton didn't appear on the *dossier*. Only Lang. The next of kin was Lang, a younger brother — presumably the chap now in South Africa. That I remember because, when the Brussels story got through to London and I had supplemented it, there was a high-level decision on how much should be told. Obviously it would do no good, and might do great harm, to tell the next of kin about Brussels and the River Line. So Heron was reported as having escaped from his prison — there were plenty of other ways of our knowing that — and as missing afterwards. . . . The names Lang and Barton didn't link in my mind until three minutes ago. That was new. You have to accept that or we shall talk at cross-purposes.

PHILIP

(*More calmly*)

Very well. I accept it. I'm sorry I flared up. (*Then he flares up again.*) My God, though, you and Marie must have thought me a pretty fool! Coming here, all agog to chatter about 'our Blaise adventure', and understanding not the first thing about it! There was I, the complete sucker, rather proud of myself for having been 'professional' enough to save the River Line from an enemy agent and to kill the man who— (*He breaks off in shame and indignation.*) And there were you and Marie, smiling at me up your sleeves, letting me babble on, allowing me day by day to——

JULIAN

Steady!

PHILIP

Well, isn't it so?

JULIAN

No, it is not.

PHILIP

Anyhow, you saw fit not to tell me — you and Marie.

JULIAN

I couldn't tell you. . . . And Marie has nothing to do with it. (*He leans across the table, taut with anxiety.*) At any moment, Marie may come out. If she does, keep your mouth shut. And keep that photograph out of sight. (*His own hand has been covering it. He pushes it across.*) Put it away now.

PHILIP

Take it. Do what you like with it.

JULIAN

(*Drawing it back under his hand, flat on the table.*) I'm sorry to be excitable. To see that photograph within Marie's reach shakes me.

PHILIP

Are you telling me that she still believes that Heron was false?

JULIAN

Yes.

PHILIP

And you have let her go on believing it for four years.   It seems mad to me.

JULIAN

(*With tired patience*)

Does it?   You forget that I love her. . . . And it hasn't been four years.   I had no contact with her from the night we left Blaise until the war ended.   I found her in a Swiss hospital with the marks of Ravensbrück still on her.   I had more or less taken it for granted that she'd know as much as I did, but she didn't.   I assumed that River Line headquarters would have had the truth from England and have told her, but they hadn't.   It may be they didn't know themselves ;   more likely, she was captured too soon.   I don't know.   I don't care. I didn't rush my fences, and it dawned on me——

PHILIP

And yet we know that she herself had a negative report from the cryptographers on Heron's letter.

JULIAN

She did indeed.   It was her telling me that in the way she told it which gave me warning that she knew nothing else.   Alone, it went for nothing either way, and she let it go for nothing.   There she was, propped up in bed, great scars on her face, eyes like black holes in a skull, wrists like matches — I can tell you, the subject of

Heron's death wasn't one for me to plunge into. And,
anyhow (*a lightened, mocking tone*), as you know, Philip
— you have cursed me for it often enough — I have a
habit of not being the first to talk. So I held my hand
and left her to lead. . . . She didn't lead — or avoid.
She talked about Heron sometimes, always with admira-
tion, as one does speak calmly and dispassionately of the
dead ; she talked of him as of someone . . . above the
battle, who had to die, but was exempt from judgement.
Not a hint of knowing that she and I — and you — had
been wrong. And gradually it dawned on me that she
really didn't know. . . . Thank God. . . . I wouldn't
tell. It would be wanton cruelty to tell. If I can do
nothing else, I can keep my mouth shut. . . . Well ?
Do you still blame me ?

PHILIP

No. The cases are different.

JULIAN

What cases ?

PHILIP

Yours and mine. Your marrying with . . . that
silence, and my — not asking.

JULIAN

Is that what happened this morning ?

PHILIP

I — quite suddenly — didn't ask.

141

PHILIP

But you will?

JULIAN

No.

PHILIP

But she understands nothing.   You must ask.

JULIAN

No, Julian.

PHILIP

Nor tell her?

JULIAN

Wouldn't that be towards her, too . . . 'wanton cruelty'?

PHILIP

If you and she love each other, it is a thousand times more cruel not to marry her.   The world is what it is. We are lonely animals.

JULIAN

Do you mean I should marry without telling her?

PHILIP

I did.

JULIAN

And have lived with — a silence between you ever since.   Isn't that true?

PHILIP

We have lived together. . . . Oh, Philip, the world is a desert until we build ourselves a roof. . . . *She* has been happy, I think. . . . Why is it impossible that you——?

142

PHILIP

For the moment, leave me out. My responsibility is all my own. I judged Heron. I gave that envelope to Chassaigne. Your responsibility is secondary. Such as it is, you and Marie share it.

JULIAN

There you are wrong. If Marie knew, she would see the whole responsibility as hers. It was my knife, but it was her order.

PHILIP

You are bitterly consistent.

JULIAN

Just consistent. . . .

PHILIP

And you mean to go on like this for ever — always afraid that some poor fool like me will blurt it out.

JULIAN

Who could? Frewer's dead.

PHILIP

Always afraid, then, to talk to her of the one subject which, because you daren't speak of it, grows bigger and bigger in your mind. Is that possible?

JULIAN

It hasn't proved impossible yet.

PHILIP

Happy?

JULIAN

Happy! Happy! Happy! You talk like the mob.

PHILIP

Who are the mob?

JULIAN

Those who wish to be happy at other men's expense!
Wherever two or three are gathered together in self-pity,
there is the mob.

PHILIP

I still ask : Are you happy?

JULIAN

We farm our land.

PHILIP

Even if Marie did assume the whole responsibility,
isn't she strong enough?

JULIAN
(*Roused to fierce retaliation*)

Isn't that a question you had better ask yourself? It
needs courage to take risks with other people's lives. It
needs a courage which — Quiet! (MARIE *has come in.*)

MARIE

No post yet?

JULIAN

No, but——

144

MARIE

What's the matter with you, Julian? (*Looking from one to the other.*) What have you been saying, you two? I heard your voices.

JULIAN

What did you hear?

MARIE

Raised voices. . . . Nothing.

JULIAN

Listen, Marie. (*He is turning the photograph-case over and over in his hands.*) I have this. You had better see it. (*She looks at the photograph, not with visible shock but with searching interest.*)

JULIAN

He was an English officer. He was an officer of the Hussars. You had better know.

MARIE

Oh, Julian! (*She sits, trembling. The photograph falls. She keeps her eyes on* JULIAN, *takes his hand, pulls herself up close to him.*) So terribly long! (*It is a cry of relief.*) Poor Julian, this is new to you.

JULIAN

No. I might have told you long ago. I thought I had the guts to keep my mouth shut. I haven't, that's all.

MARIE

My dearest, it is not new to me.

JULIAN

Not new!   How did you know?

MARIE

From Brussels.   Just before I was taken.

JULIAN

Tell me, then——

MARIE

Not now.   I don't want to talk now.   Oh, Julian!

JULIAN

But if all this time——

MARIE

Not now.   Not yet.   (*She puts up her arms and kisses him.*)   All words are dangerous.

Curtain

ACT III

SCENE 2

The same.   After   dinner   that   night.   MARIE *and* PHILIP *discovered.*

PHILIP

She will not come.

MARIE

If not, you must go to her.

PHILIP

No, Marie.

MARIE

You are *naïf*, Philip.   I am not.   Both ways one can be self-deceived.

PHILIP

Naïve?   My mother says : 'guileless'.

MARIE

I wonder whether you have ever asked yourself why people are fond of you — people quite different from one another and miles apart from you. . . . Or why, if it comes to that, Valerie loves you.   She does, you know.

PHILIP

I know.   At least——

MARIE

Don't qualify it !   One knows that it is so or that

147

it is not. One knows by the touch of a hand, the feel of the air. I know that Heron did not love me. And you know that Valerie — but do you know why? Do you in the least know what is lovable in you? It is the fact that you don't know. You are loved because, in that respect, you are without vanity. The miracle happens because, to you, it always is a miracle. People are desired who expect to be desired, and envied who expect to be envied, but no one is ever deeply loved who is not as incredulous of love as he is of death. Julian and I have been happier to-day than ever in the past. We love each other without silences now and — yes — with all our hearts, such as they are. But our love is limited by our personalities. There are great lovers as there are great poets, and we are not among them. I shall never be greatly loved because my intellect is too quick: I am not *naïve* enough. For the same reason my father, poet though he was, must always have fallen short of being a supreme poet; his poetry never took his own breath away; he was never incredulous of what appeared on his paper. He knew precisely how it came there; he knew the reason for everything; so do I — even for love, and so I shall never be loved as you are loved, and I shall never — oh well, let it go.

PHILIP

Say what you were going to say, Marie.

MARIE

I shall never know how to die as Heron died. Do you understand that?

PHILIP

No.

MARIE

I have not wonder enough. It is the grace to receive
Grace. Not granted to me. Do you understand that?

PHILIP

Perhaps, in time, I might understand if——

MARIE

Ah, don't try. Don't have the killing arrogance to
try. That is my own intellectual sin.

PHILIP

(*Who has been looking out over the valley*)
I think she won't come.

MARIE

Your mind goes back! How rightly and simply!

PHILIP

And if she does, it will only be because not to come
might create an . . . awkwardness greater than her
coming. You know, Marie, she has that too in common
with her brother. I can't imagine circumstances in which
Heron would ever have made a scene.

MARIE

(*With a smile*)
That might have told us that he was English. . . .
Philip, don't walk about. Come and sit beside me. I
have something to say. . . . (*He moves towards her.*)

149

Upon what happens or does not happen to-night, not your life only but her life depends.

PHILIP

Are you suggesting, as Julian did, that I should marry without telling her? (*He sits beside her.*)

MARIE

Did Julian say that?

PHILIP

He said in effect : 'Keep your mouth shut. Marry. Do as I did.'

MARIE

That was foolish. You are incapable of doing as he did. (*Touching his hand affectionately*) You have not . . . the gift of reticence. . . . No, that is not what I suggest. But is there any reason that Valerie should not be told and allowed to judge for herself?

PHILIP

I think there is.

MARIE

What you did, you did unknowingly. Are you to blame?

PHILIP

Do you really believe that only the sins we commit knowingly are to be expiated and forgiven?

MARIE

Isn't that the accepted modern code?

PHILIP

It is the accepted modern avoidance. You don't believe it yourself. The whole of Greek tragedy denies it. (JULIAN *comes in, turns up the lamp, and quietly listens.*) Go to Fate and say: 'Please, I didn't know! Please, I didn't mean it!' A man may let you off. Fate won't.

MARIE

If there is such a thing as Fate.

PHILIP

Very well, go to Nature and say: 'I didn't understand! I didn't intend!' Nature will flick you away like a dead fly.

MARIE

Even the Greeks sometimes allowed man to be reconciled with the gods. Tragedy doesn't always demand catastrophe finally ruinous. It isn't compassionless.

JULIAN

No. But the terms of its compassion are inexorable.

PHILIP

(*Going his own way*)

That's what I mean. You can't cry off. You have to bear responsibility for the wrong that came through you until you are . . . purified of it. Absolved. In my case, how else than by silence?

JULIAN

My God, you have changed.

151   M

PHILIP

Yes, I have changed. But I am not seeing myself as the hero of a Greek tragedy, believe me. I am only a little teacher trying to be honest — a little boaster whose pet melodrama has caught him in a trap.

MARIE

(*Firmly*)

It is her life as well as yours. May not she decide for herself?

PHILIP

Oh, Marie, do not torment me! You speak as if there were only she and I. It isn't a question of what she decides or I decide. Our marriage is . . . prohibited . . . by Heron's death. . . . Prohibited, do you understand?

MARIE

No. I do not. Of course, if she were told, she might feel that it was intolerable to be the wife of the man who was responsible . . . who was partly responsible . . . for killing her brother. That you must risk. But the decision is one that she is entitled to make for herself.

PHILIP

It is not one that she can make or that I can make. The prohibition is not hers or mine. It is absolute. Its origin is not in either of us; it is in him. My responsibility is to him; my debt, not repayable. He alone might have forgiven it.

MARIE

You are binding yourself to the dead.

PHILIP

I don't feel it so. If I did, I should not be bound.
He is alive for her. He is always alive for me — above
all, here. From the first evening in this house — in the
place that he might have had at your table; among us
on this lawn — among us now. And quite unspeakably
alive in *her*, as though he were looking out from the
windows of her eyes.

MARIE

(*After a long pause*)

Ah, my poor Philip, if it is *in her* you see him, then
I have no more to say. (VALERIE *comes out of the shadows
at the back of the stage.* JULIAN *sees her first and rises;*
PHILIP *next. The ensuing scene opens fast and lightly.
They are talking at haphazard. Anything to keep talk on a
level that is not dangerous.*)

JULIAN

You have climbed the hill alone? Come in.

VALERIE

Godmother has been helping me pack. She was
tired and has gone to bed. (*She sits. Lays her hand
against the side of her face, then draws it down to take the
coffee that is being offered her.*)

VALERIE

Thank you, Philip. (*To* MARIE) I must stay only a
little while. I have an early start. Really, I only came
to say good-bye and because——

MARIE

All your packing is done?

VALERIE

Except the very last things.

MARIE

Then you can be peaceful here a little while. . . .
At any rate, your last evening in the English country
will be spent among friends all of whom . . . love you.
May I say that?

VALERIE

Thank you. . . . Who was it, in your Revolution
I think, who on the night before he was guillotined
looked out of his window and said — and now I can't
remember. Isn't it absurd and humiliating how the
thread of what you were saying, quite suddenly, snaps?
When it happens I feel always as if someone had come
up behind me and taken . . . do you see what I mean?
. . . and taken the telephone out of my hand.

MARIE

Listen! (*A silence.*)

PHILIP

You said that as if you were hearing music.

MARIE

I was hearing nothing. How still the night is. I
used to have the idea when I was a little girl that, if
ever there was *no* sound, not even the turning of a leaf,
nothing, then time stopped too; no one died, no one
was born, no one grew older. I used to hold my breath.

(*Silence.*) Oh, but one has to breathe again and pour out coffee and light cigarettes. . . . Give me a cigarette.

JULIAN

You never smoke.

MARIE

(*Taking a cigarette from* PHILIP)

Never mind.

VALERIE

What I meant about the telephone was—— (*The others are all in movement as she begins to speak.* MARIE *has lifted the coffee-pot. Now she sets it down.* PHILIP *is offering the flame of his cigarette lighter.*)

MARIE

No, I won't smoke. (JULIAN *has been idly putting together a little pile of books at the side of his chair, stooping down to them. Now he comes up and listens. They all freeze to listen as* VALERIE *continues:*)

VALERIE

That often when memory snaps over something utterly unimportant as mine did just now, I feel as if someone behind me — or someone *in* me perhaps — had said : 'Do stop talking nonsense. Do get off the line. I have something real to say. Do let me talk on your line.' . . . And then I stop. . . . I suppose when I get to South Africa that will be a complete break. New scenes. New interests. A complete break. I don't know. That is what . . . frightens me a little.

PHILIP

Still, one often imagines a place — the feel of it

155

anyhow — without having formed a describable picture of it. I do. And it's the same with people. Reading history or old letters, I often get a perfectly clear idea of a person without having a notion of what he looks like.

VALERIE

It's true of stories. I read a description and take it in and accept it, and yet at the same time the action may go on in a scene of my own childhood — Ophelia in our garden at home or the Old Guard at Waterloo advancing up a hill called Cumberfield Down — and it works! It isn't incongruous. I don't know why. Marie shall tell us.

MARIE

(*Avoiding dangerous ground*)

Why do you ask me?

PHILIP

(*Plunging*)

Julian and Marie never answer questions if they can avoid it. But I can tell you why it isn't incongruous that Ophelia should be in Denmark and in your garden at the same time. At least, I think I can. Isn't it because a place or a person can have being in our minds without having physical existence there? (VALERIE *rises.*)

JULIAN

Which on the face of it is odd, unless you go much further and say that identity is independent of physical character.

PHILIP

Which, in the experience of it, is true.

VALERIE
(*Withdrawn a little now, close to the stone seat*)
If that is true of the living, it must be true of those
we say are dead. You must feel it of Heron, as I do of
my brother. (JULIAN *gets up.*)

JULIAN
Isn't it best to let the whole thing go?

VALERIE
I'm sorry. I meant to this evening. We did talk at
first of quite casual things. (*Under stress, she moves away
upstage.* JULIAN *follows her.* PHILIP *also would have gone
to her, but* MARIE *lays a restraining hand on his arm.*)

MARIE
Philip, you must help her by telling her.

PHILIP
If that was ever possible, it is now too late.

MARIE
It is terrible that she should remain ignorant of what
we all know. She speaks of Heron and her brother as
different people. She speaks quietly of her brother in
the presence of us who killed him. We can't sit here
and let her do that. If you will not tell her, I must.

PHILIP
You can't, Marie, without my permission.

MARIE
That is true.

157

PHILIP

And you will not. You have . . . the gift of reticence. . . . Be patient. There is something in *her*
to-night that I have never seen before. You must not
disturb it. She is possessed, but not yet fully.

MARIE

Possessed ?

PHILIP

Not by an evil spirit. . . . By an interior grace. It
is — look at her now.

VALERIE

He has been in my mind all day — this evening more
and more. It was that, really, which, just after I came,
made me forget what I was trying to say. It was he
who . . . took the receiver out of my hand. It did
seem then that he was standing behind me. . . . And
now. (*She looks slowly at them all, one by one, but none
speaks, and she continues:*) To-morrow it will be
different. There will be a broken day in London, I
know, but this is really my last night in England, the
one at any rate that I shall remember as the last. If he
had been alive I shouldn't have been going, and there
was a time this morning when I felt that my going was
a new separation from him — a kind of desertion. Now,
I don't feel that, but more as if——

PHILIP

As if he were here !

VALERIE

More, even, than that. . . . (*Wrenching herself back*

to normality, with change of tone and speed, to JULIAN)
I'm sorry. It must be tiresome of me to speak like this
of someone you and Marie have never known. Philip
and I have talked of him so much that— (*To* JULIAN)
How I wish that you had known him too!

JULIAN

I—— (*He shifts, starts up, and while she continues,
strides upstage in nervous agitation, returning to midstage
in time for his next speech.*)

VALERIE
(*Calmly*)

Not that the appearance of anyone matters ultimately,
I suppose. Anyhow, one can't communicate it. If in
my ship, two or three days from now, I were speaking
of this evening to some stranger and tried to describe
Philip so that the stranger should have a picture of him
in his mind, I should fail utterly. The eyes, the mouth,
the nose, the shape of the head — yes, all that, all the
separate bits, but never the whole appearance recogniz-
ably. Language simply doesn't provide.

JULIAN
(*Vehemently*)

Nor does thought. Not only will you be unable,
two or three nights hence, to describe Philip's face but
you will be unable to see it. Look away now! Look
out there, over the other valley! (*He points. She looks
straight out over the audience.*) Can you see his face
distinctly, clearly, completely, as you do when your
eyes are on it? Can you?

VALERIE

I can see *him*!

JULIAN

But his face, his features?

VALERIE

No, not as one sees with one's eyes. Or even in a photograph. But *him* I can see. (*She turns back to them.*) Of course Philip knows what my brother looked like. He has a photograph.

JULIAN

(*Steadily*)

Marie and I know what he looked like. We——

MARIE

(*On her feet*)

Valerie——

PHILIP

Be patient. Wait. (PHILIP *and* MARIE *and* JULIAN *have spoken almost together. The secret is almost out.* MARIE *goes defensively to* JULIAN'S *side. But* VALERIE *goes on quietly :*)

VALERIE

You have seen the photograph?

MARIE

Yes, Philip showed it to us. (*And the danger is past.*)

VALERIE

I'm glad. Not that it tells anything. I'm glad, all the same, that you have seen it. . . . My trouble — I mean the stubborn part of it, the bit I couldn't dis-

entangle — was : I didn't know how he died. He just
vanished. I didn't even know in what country — in
Germany, perhaps, or Belgium. It was a long time
before I felt sure it was in France.

JULIAN

How were you sure? What proof was there of that?

VALERIE

None. . . . Of course no proof. (*She has picked up
some leaves and now, rubbing them, lets the fragments fall
from her hands.*) Not in the least to know how he died
was for a time a bleak gap in my knowledge of him. It
prevented me from being with him imaginatively as he
died. As though I had abandoned him. I couldn't help
trying to see the place and trying to go to it — sometimes it was a field, or a black, muddy street, or a brick
cell with a bare electric bulb — but it was all false, I
knew it inside me ; images of loneliness, that was all.
. . . And sometimes, as a corrective, I used to imagine
that he died among friends who had learned to know
and love him.

MARIE

That may have been true.

VALERIE

And that he hadn't the shudder of loneliness when
he died. (*Very slowly, feeling for the last word*) Only a
moment, perhaps, of (*looking at* MARIE)—incredulity. . . .
But that is long ago — my trying and trying to picture
the scene and revisit it. That is all past. . . . I was
completely wrong. The way in which he died was not,

for him, of the least importance. (*And now she begins to speak with an authority not her own. She is no longer speculating or feeling her way. She is narrating facts.*) When he was dying and those who killed him watched him die. . . . (*She breaks off, rises quickly, moves away from them, listens, returns.*)

Wait.   It is not she who is speaking now.

VALERIE

Even when his body was dead and a foot . . . jabbed at his body. . . . You see, there was no question of his forgiving or not forgiving them.   They bore their responsibility in the predicament of the world.   Blame and forgiveness he was leaving behind.   All our debts and credits were emptied out.   He let them go — (*She falters.*)   He let them — (*She falters.*)   I let them go. They went quite naturally, as sleep goes when one wakes or waking goes when one sleeps, easily and simply.   Just for a moment, between waking and sleeping, I was . . . incredulous that they should go so easily, afterwards not. Without   wrench,   without   struggle — 'loss   without losing'. . . . Who said that?

PHILIP

(*Close to her*)

'Loss without losing' — who said that?

VALERIE

My   brother   did. . . . Heron   did.   (*She rises as understanding flows into her and looks, puzzled at first, from face to face.*) You . . . and you . . . and you . . . and he! Ah! (*She sways and covers her face with her hands.* PHILIP, *thinking she is about to fall, holds her*) No. I am not falling. It is only that I am a little tired. . . . (*She sits. For a moment,* JULIAN *and* MARIE *watch her.*)

MARIE

For me, and Julian too, the word we cling to — only Heron could have spoken it, is: 'They bore their responsibility in the predicament of the world'. That is the condition of amnesty for all our generation. The only one, I think.

VALERIE

Did *I* say that? (MRS. MURIVEN *comes in up-Left.*)

MRS. MURIVEN

I am old but, as you see, extremely energetic.

MARIE

We thought you were in bed.

MRS. MURIVEN

I was. But I am not. We all spend too long in bed. I thought suddenly: up there life is going on. It is quite a short hill. I will go and see. The time will come when that may not be possible.

MARIE

But you are tired. Look, this is a comfortable chair.

JULIAN

The party begins again. Look. This is your own Delamain — Oh Six.

MRS. MURIVEN

Thank you. A little glass. . . . But it is cold here.

MARIE

Then shall we carry it in? (JULIAN, MARIE, *and* MRS. MURIVEN *go out, but at the entrance to the drawing-room* MRS. MURIVEN *pauses and says:*)

MRS. MURIVEN

Do you remember that ridiculous Russian who wrote plays? I thought it was all nonsense. But it isn't. My little dog really does eat nuts.

VALERIE

(*When alone with* PHILIP)

Was it that — that Heron and my brother were the same — which you would not tell me?

PHILIP

Yes, Valerie.

VALERIE

Would you never have told me? Why, Philip?

PHILIP

Some day I will tell you the reasons. Not now. I was imprisoned by the past; now I am free. I was guilty and now — oh it isn't easy to say.

VALERIE

Does it need saying? Be at peace; my dear, be at peace.

PHILIP

I think it does need saying. In a way, it is the treaty

between us. It is not that you have forgiven me. I was guilty and am innocent, as though I had been reborn. The solution of tragedy, I suppose, can never come from outside, but only from a power within the tragedy itself. If this morning I had told you and asked to be forgiven, and you had forgiven me, it would have been meaningless. Sin can't be cancelled by sharing it. Nor can truth. Our knowledge would have been like a locked room in our house. We should have tried every key, I suppose — reason, tolerance, plain oblivion — and they would have seemed to turn. But the room would still have been locked. That is why I didn't tell.

VALERIE

One cannot shut one's eyes to things not seen with eyes. . . . As it is . . .

PHILIP

As it is?

VALERIE

Peace, my dearest love.

PHILIP

Between us?

VALERIE

And between us and him.

PHILIP

Valerie, speak of him openly. I don't know how much you yourself recognize of what happened this evening. I must know. For me, when you were letting little pieces of leaf and stick fall through your hands, you were Heron; it was an interior grace.

VALERIE

I saw nothing and heard nothing.

PHILIP

Saw! Heard! That isn't what I was asking. That precisely is *not* — one doesn't see or hear what is inside oneself.

VALERIE

Then I can answer your question. The rest is true. If you mean that, this evening, he was within me — yes, that is true. And you had the grace to receive it. Otherwise it would not have been true. That is the . . . the absolution we have received together.

PHILIP

From him.

VALERIE

Through him. Through me, perhaps, because I love you. No man absolves. But, through him, there is absolution. Innocence has come to us.

PHILIP

But I killed him.

VALERIE

No, my dear, you did not. You could not. There is peace between us and him.

Curtain

PRINTED BY R. & R. CLARK, LTD., EDINBURGH

/